The Life Left to Live

by William Gannon

This book is dedicated to those who added so many meaningful moments in my life and the many other people's lives as well. Although you were all taken from us too soon, you all live in my heart and head until we meet again.

Marc Izzo

Matt Escoto

Jerry Lunney

William Gannon

Mary Lunney

Jay Escoto

Joe Kuczo

Danielle Gannon

William James Gannon

Agnes Z. Gannon

Mike Terzi

Maryanne Gannon

Charles Graeb

Isabelle Gannon

Leon Z. Klopocki

Joe Roche

Pete Femniak

Foreword

Each of us is obliged to travel a life path, a crooked, unpredictable road that includes a good measure of happiness and a portion of pain. Many people face this obligation with an "I'll take what comes" attitude, and take a hands-free approach to life. We all face difficulties, and some fall victim to tribulations, at times surrendering to the emotional and physical obstacles that periodically mar our way. For Bill Gannon, however, assuming a laissez faire approach to life was, and remains, unacceptable.

Bill Gannon is recognized as one of the most courageous citizens of Wallingford, Connecticut. The youngest sibling to four older sisters and the son of William and MaryAnne Gannon, Bill has been a whirlwind of energy and service to his community, loved ones and friends.

The landscape of the life articulated in this book is one of catastrophic circumstances. A handsome, charming, and talented young man, Bill was on the fast-track to a Division I athletic scholarship. On January 20, 1989, he was involved in a disastrous car accident that ultimately claimed the lives of two of his closest friends and left Bill permanently disabled. Though initially told he would never walk again, through his character, unity of purpose, and limitless fortitude, he proved his doctors wrong. That same accident opened the door for Bill to meet his future wife, Agnes. The couple had four children, sons Billy Jr. and Jeremy, and daughters Casey and Danielle. Tragically, they lost Danielle due to complications at birth. The ensuing years proved to be just as difficult for Bill, as he lost his father, his beloved wife Agnes, and then his devoted mother.

It has been one of life's privileges to have known Bill since he was a budding youth athlete with undeniable promise for the future. Following the devastating accident that claimed his pro football career, Bill has refused to give in to self-pity. I have been in awe of his inner strength.

In one of the most dramatic moments I have ever seen, Bill put on his high school football jersey one more time, playing quarterback and despite his injuries completed a pass before leaving the gridiron on his terms in 1989, his senior year of high school. No one who witnessed that moment of courage and determination failed to be moved … for a lifetime.

Tragedy in some manifestation touches every person's life at some point, however the manner in which Bill Gannon has met and continues to address adversity, living a life of blessed happiness and fulfillment is what makes this book a must read. Bill walks in victory every day of his life and is a living example of how one can meet and overcome adversity

Stephen W. Hoag, Ph.D.

Coach Hoag (left) and author Bill Gannon (right) at a ceremony honoring Bill's father at the Lyman Hall Hall of Fame

Preface

Where there's a will there's a way! Where's there's a will there's a way! It's worth saying twice. Life is too short to be bitter when you can be better. Bad things happen to us all and how we deal with them can keep us down or lift us up into a new or different direction. Sometimes you just need to find yourself again. Either way, any way you have to, find a way to make yourself happy again. Return to the things that make you happy. If you need to find new things to find fulfillment, then find them. Push yourself to that new purpose and find the inner strength you didn't think you had. It's in there. It's just waiting for you to call on it. Why wait in sorrow or sulk in darkness when you don't need to? Find people, places, or activities that return your smile, your happiness. Don't surround yourself in sorrow. I hope this book helps you rediscover, or maybe redefine, your life. There are times when I made the impossible possible, you can too. Why is it so easy to fall back on worry? It's said practice makes perfect so why can't we get beyond the worry and welcome healing. Is healing a harder step, it doesn't have to be. I've been successful because I've learned to change my thought process. I chose not to linger in loss, but find meaning in my life again. I hope my stories and techniques can help you as well. Let's get your journey going.

Acknowledgments

I would like to thank all the men and women from the emergency services who got us out of the car and to the hospital that fateful night in 1989. They gave us a chance to fight for our lives.

To the doctors, nurses, and hospital staff who all aided in our recovery, thank you.

To my friends and family members who had my back during my football comeback, thank you all for your continued support.

To my high school English teachers, Mrs. Cannata, Mrs. Toman, Mrs. Grady, and Mr. Mannion, thank you for pushing me to better myself as a student and person.

To Cindi Pietrzyk, who edits my book and makes me look good.

To all the people who take that next step when others don't think it's possible. Keep going, you are an inspiration.

Introduction

For those of you who haven't read my last book, *To Lose But Not Fail,* let me tell you a little bit about me. In my life I've had to deal with a lot of loss and physical pain. My first memory is one of pain. I suffered a third-degree burn on the right side of my chest when I was five years old due to an unfortunate accident with boiling water. When I was ten years old I stepped on a pin, the broken pinhead traveled up my blood stream resulting in the need for emergency surgery. When I was seventeen, two of my best friends and I were involved in a motor vehicle accident. The accident claimed the life of one of my friends that January night. I sustained serious injuries that destroyed my dream of playing pro football. My other friend died a few years later from complications from the injuries he received that night.

During the next four years following the accident, I lost three out of my four grandparents. In 2001 my wife and I lost our daughter Danielle. There's nothing worse than losing a child. Later that year I lost my father. I lost my Uncle Joe, who was like a second father to me. A few years later I lost my wife to a brain aneurysm. My brother-in-law, Mike Terzi, was taken from us at the age of forty. My mother passed a few years later from cancer. My Grandmother Gannon died a few years later. My father-in-law, Leon Klopocki, died on Father's Day in 2016.

That's a lot of loss to endure, but I survived. I want to teach you that you can too. . I hope this book jump starts your recovery and gets you moving toward laughter, love, and longevity. I hope I can bring some hope to you when you are facing a situation you might think is hopeless. I believe I survived the accident, and my heartbreak after heartbreak for a reason. I believe I was meant to help others find their way through their own pain.

In this book, I discuss my approach to recovery. While everyone's recovery will look different, I believe if you follow my approach loosely, at your own pace, you will find happiness again.

The first step in any recovery is facing the loss, feeling the pain and accepting your loss.

The next step in recovery is moving past your loss. This doesn't mean forgetting who or what you have lost, but learning to live your new normal without them. Whether this means living with a physical disability or without a loved one, once you have faced your loss, accepted your loss, you will be ready to move into your new life and find joy and happiness once again. You will focus on what you have, not what you have lost. Remember I'm not a doctor. I've got my training and knowledge from life. I have been successful because I was able to shift my way of thinking. You will smile again, you will love again, you will live again. You can do it, and when you are ready, you will. Read on to find out how.

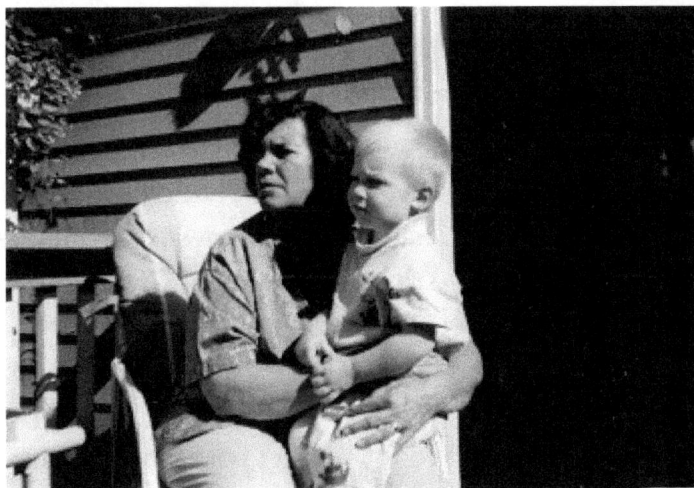

My mother and nephew Billy Graeb

Learning To Live Again

Let the lessons of yesterday strengthen the love of today.

It is easy to appreciate the people or things we have lost, but why do we so often forget to do this when they are still with us? We take for granted the time we are given to spend with our loved ones. It is only when they are gone that we truly realize and appreciate that gift. Time with loved ones is invaluable, so why does it take a loss for us to fully recognize that? Are we programmed to live life like this? No. This is a choice we make. I heard someone once say that we are just a dash between two dates. I believe we are more than that. Some of us are blessed to bring other lives into this world, but we all have gifts to offer to better the world around us, even to better the people around us. When I was growing up, I saw that my grandparents held onto things, reused them, repurposed them, fixed them. Things weren't disposable like they are today. People of my grandparents' generation respected the value of things and always looked for a way to make the most of them. This not only applied to physical things, but also to people and relationships. My grandparents and others of that time period held close those they loved, they put effort into relationships, and found ways to make them work. Today, I believe we give up on things and people too quickly. We toss things away too soon, instead of working at them or repurposing them and finding a way to fit them into our lives. We've become too much of an easy come easy go society. I think it's time we revisit this philosophy and maybe take a page or two from our grandparents' world.

Today, everything has to be fast. We want that instant gratification. We lose interest too quickly in things that don't pay off immediately. We have lost patience. I can't see how that can sustain itself. I think one only gets better with time and experience. Sure, Lady Luck can change that equation once in a while, but for the most part, change and gratification takes grit and determination. Patience is one of the greatest lessons we can learn. Be thankful for what you have as you work toward what you want. Focusing on the things you have accomplished instead of worrying about what you haven't. I am not saying settle for less, but to shoot for the stars. Keep your eye on where you want to be, and never lose track of where you come from. Appreciate what you have earned and learned along the way.

Stop and celebrate milestones along the way as you strive to accomplish your major goals. Envision yourself accomplishing those goals. Put in the blood, sweat, and tears to get there. People will notice and help you along the way. It's not difficult to notice who has the passion and who's there for the paycheck.

I'm not saying it will be easy. Nothing worth having ever is. If you're anything like me, you won't like it when your life takes an unexpected turn, which it undoubtedly will. I love having a routine I can stick to. So when my life gets altered or pushed in a new direction, it certainly is not what I want, but these changes and unexpected detours are something we all have to deal with and address.. Throughout my life, I've come to realize that love and laughter are better allies than crying and despairing. Life is about balance, so you can look back and mourn, but you also have to then look into the future. That is what has worked for me.

This book is about sharing the lessons I have learned. Did I reach every goal I wanted to achieve? Of course not, but that doesn't mean I have failed. Just like those things our grandparents held on to, sometimes your life just needs a different purpose and it's never, ever something you should throw away. Always give back.

Shoot for the Stars

"Surround yourself with positive people who will support you when it rains, not just when it shines."

—Unknown

My faith asks me to forgive, and that is fine. I will forgive, but I will not forget. I will give you both cheeks to slap, but the third strike you are out. I refuse to waste time or energy on people who only care about themselves or look to cause problems for others. Instead, I focus on the ones who care about me and the ones I love. This is my advice to you, too.

In my life, I have found money to be the great divider. Nothing can drive a wedge like the almighty dollar. As singer Neil Diamond says, "Money talks, but it don't sing and dance, and it don't walk."

Surround yourself with people who value your company. Make the most of the time spent together and you will find that the long time between your visits does not matter. Recently, I caught up with some friends from high school. We had a great visit and we all walked away that day feeling as if we hadn't missed a beat. We picked up right where we left off all those years ago. Some people choose to lose or let go of their past, but I have chosen to learn from mine. Reconnecting with those people from your past who value you and bring happiness to your life now is a good thing. For those in your past who are negative, doubtful, bad news people who only want information from you for their own gain? Leave them there. You need to see these people for who they really are. While everyone has a bad day here or there, those people who are constantly bringing you down will strangle the life out of you.

Find the activities or people that bring fulfillment into your life. Don't allow people to ruin your self-perception. Don't let people control you or your mind. Find people who support you and your dreams. People come into our lives to point us in certain directions. Some people influence us to go in a positive direction, and some in a not-so-positive direction, but which direction we choose is ultimately up to us.

There is nothing wrong with shooting for the stars as long as you prepare yourself for falls along the way and recognize the fight you will have to go through to get to where you want to be. Never lose sight of your end goal. Believe in yourself and your abilities. Give everything you have, push yourself to your breaking point, then push that breaking point to a new level. Always finish what you start. If you do not believe in yourself, why should others? Finish what you start.

Criticism will come, often in two forms. The first one is positive, it is called constructive criticism, a simple exercise that is used to better yourself by making improvements. Hurtful criticism is different and you need to get it off your back where it will only weigh you down. I used it as fuel to finish my goal. When I was making my comeback to football I'd say for every person who supported me there were five who didn't. Here's part of a letter written by a doctor who wanted to amputate my leg the night of the accident.

I respect Dr. Bradburn and Dr. Palermo. However common sense is definitely not their forte. High school sports has come full circle when a Cheshire football coach instructs his lineman not to tackle the gasser. William lacks mobility, agility and capability to withstand a competitive aggressive tackle. This is not a question of healing it is a simple question of total football disability. All the coaches in the Housatonic league recognize this disability.

The dream of Mr. and Mrs. William Gannon and their son are painfully a memory left on Thanksgiving Day in 1988. Their football coach, trainers and apparently their physicians, Dr. Palermo and Dr. Bradburn were all wrong! William belongs on the sideline and not in any game situation. How else can we protect this student athlete? How can we protect the opposition lineman from the psychological trauma of perhaps seriously injuring an already permanently disabled athlete?

The doctor never saw me after that night. He never evaluated my charts or my physical status; he knew nothing about me. Dr. Palermo had a linebacker from Penn State (a division-one athlete) who repeatedly hit me, so I knew what I could take. I knew I wasn't the same player, but I did everything I needed to do to be out there. Every player was wearing a label on their helmet and every year a coach read that warning to us. Any player at any time can injure someone permanently. Football is a contact sport and the risks are there for everyone who puts on a uniform. I can promise you that no one was more prepared to be hurt than I. For some reason this doctor wanted his opinion known. Maybe it was because I didn't remain under his treatment that January night. Every moment of pain was worth every minute I was on the verge of something amazing, and this man's words weren't going to get the best of me.

Both Dr. Palermo and Dr. Bradburn laughed at the letter and my parents wanted me to stick to the plans. I guess I was held to a higher standard by the people in my corner. This goal was greater than one person and impossible to accomplish on my own. The best advice I can give is to not take the bait when people throw it out there. Some people can't recognize your talent, they can't measure your heart just by looking at you. Set your sights for your goals and go after them. Don't waste your time on distractions. It will test your discipline, but you must pick your own battles. We can surround ourselves with negative thoughts or positive thoughts.

Both my father and my Uncle Joe, taught me how to block things out of my mind and focus on the task at hand. This is one of those traits worth its weight in gold. You see, criticism of me didn't stop with the doctors. The girl responsible for the accident had a stepfather who ran a large company. He instructed his employees to write to the newspaper and bash me and the people around me. I didn't have a problem with them riding me, but when they brought the others into the mix, you worry for them. When these things happen to you, you need to see that the goal is bigger than the grief. I had great people surrounding me. People who believed in me. My Uncle Joe would tell me all the time to work on my weaknesses. That advice was huge because we never really think about doing this. It makes us focus on our failures. It's never fun to consistently mess up time and time again, until that one day when the tide turns and the failures turn into success. You need to pick your battles and you will eventually win the war.

Living Your New Normal

"If you cannot be grateful for what you have received, then be thankful for what you have been spared."

Yiddish proverb

About six months before my car accident, I was delivering restaurant equipment with my father. This gentleman came out to lend a hand. I noticed a pronounced limp, so I asked if he was all right. He went on to tell me how he had been in a car accident and had to learn to walk again. I was perplexed by what I had just heard. We learn to walk as babies, is that something we forget?

Curiosity got the best of me. "How do you forget how to walk?" I asked. He explained that he hadn't forgotten how to walk but due to his injuries he had to learn a new way to walk. He'd had to adapt to his new circumstances. Only seventeen at the time, I didn't understand completely what he had said. Little did I know at the time just how fortuitous that conversation would be.

Simple things we take for granted, like the ability to walk, can be lost in the blink of an eye. Every day we get up and assume we will be able to perform these simple acts because we have done so time and time again. But life throws us curve balls and plunges us into new circumstances to which we need to adapt in order to survive. Often that adaptation can be difficult and challenging, but we can't give up, we must believe in ourselves and keep our eyes on the prize. The end result may not be exactly how you pictured it, but that's part of the process.

When we make it out of any incident or accident, we are considered survivors. It is a blessing to survive, however it is often a challenge to find a way to live again in our new normal. To recover quickly or even at all, you have to focus on what you could have lost, not on what you did lose. Let that sink in, and then start working with what you have, what is left. Assess your new set of circumstances, take inventory of what you have, and work with it to live your best life. Set , to achieve goals that while they may look a little different than you originally thought, still bring you happiness and peace.

In January 1989, I was in a car accident that claimed the life of my friend Marc Izzo. Marc was full of life and endless potential that so tragically ended that night. The emotional, physical, financial, and mental fallout from that night was all consuming. I had to break it down to survive it. Yes, lives were lost and those are irreplaceable. But all the other things could be repaired or at least resolved.

This is where I learned to focus on not what was lost, but what was left. People always question my faith in God. They ask how can I still believe after I have lost so much? That is easy to answer. I do not look at what I have lost. I focus on what remains. What I have in the present rather than what I had in the past. This theme will keep coming up throughout this book because I believe it's very important in any recovery.

I had dreams of becoming a professional football player. The injuries sustained in the accident stole those dreams from me, but what they didn't steal was my love of the game. The passion that God put in me for that game was what saved my life. It spurred me to work hard to get in top physical shape. It led me to lead a clean life and helped me recover at a quicker pace.

I imagine my road to recovery would have been a lot worse had I looked at everything in a negative way. Sometimes things just need to stay simple. When I was hit with a negative, I looked for ways to balance the scales or even tilt them in my favor with a positive thing or two. Life is about balance. Yes, you will have your roller coaster moments, but all in all, keep it as close to the middle as possible.

I had to accept that my chance to play professional football was gone., but I could still give to the game in other ways. This goal took an adjustment here or there, but it kept me around something I loved. It was my new normal. Life went on.

In 1990, after I had graduated high school, I was offered the opportunity to coach with Dennis Mannion for my former high school team, the Sheehan Titans. Coach Mannion was a hero of mine and I would have jumped at that opportunity had it happened any other year. But the timing was not right for two reasons. One, I was focused on being a father. Two, former teammates were still on the team, which would make me their coach. It's not that I thought my teammates wouldn't respect me, it was that I was afraid they would see me as less than who I was due to my injuries. This was just who I was at this stage of the recovery. I was still working on building myself back up, and the mental challenges were proving to be more difficult than the physical ones.

I had also made a promise to my friends in the car that night. Things were very grim just moments before the rescue teams came on site. There was one point I thought that none of us were getting out of the car alive.

In the moment when I thought I was going to die, I asked God to grant me a moment to think of all the people I loved. He not only granted me my moment, but he provided me with a lifetime and the strength to will myself in a positive direction with that newfound time. I lost opportunities, sure, but I still had my life. Like I have said, people are one of the only true losses we ever have to face. Both Marc Izzo and Matt Escoto are guys you can't replace. It was hard to find a flaw in those two guys. I received a lot of feedback from my other book about the people I included in those pages. I can only speak for me, but the stories I heard and shared were like a breath of fresh air. They brought me right back to those great times I shared with my friends. Although our time together was short, it was a true blessing.

Accepting Loss and Moving Past Grief

"That it will never come again is what makes life so sweet."

—Emily Dickinson

One of the questions I most often get asked is, "How do you deal with loss?" People want to know what the secret is to moving past the grief. What I have found is that everyone will go at their own pace to find that peace, and what works for one person may not work for another. What has worked best for me is appreciating what I have and recognizing what I have lost. Like that old saying, it is better to have loved and lost than to have never loved at all, I believe if you can appreciate the value of what you had, even if it was for a short time in your life, that is the blessing, that you had them in your life a little. Hold on to that more than the loss of them, and you will be better for it.

I will not be the guy who tells you nothing will ever go wrong. Things will go wrong, my life is a perfect example of that. Bad things are going to happen, and when they do, face the pain and find a way to overcome it. Seek out the people, the stories, and the therapy that will make you stronger and wiser. Look to those of us who have come out the other side, because that way you know it can be done. You can do it. Do not ever sell yourself short. Hope and faith are very powerful agents and can overcome doubt.

Every time I speak, people approach me after I'm done. Most times they want to share their goal or loss with me. I have heard the most heartbreaking stories, but I don't have the cure. I can only offer a road map to conquer the demons. It is up to each individual to take the torch and carry it through to his or her recovery. You cannot sleep your nightmare away, even though you may want to. It was tough to fall asleep when I finally got home from the hospital after the accident. I had a vision stuck in my head I couldn't shake at the time. I would take NyQuil just to get me to sleep. I never mentioned it to anyone because I felt I had already put so many of my loved ones through so much. The physical therapy I was doing was at a minimum of twelve hours a day and even that couldn't exhaust me into forgetting. That's when I started to notice that I needed to take charge of my issue. Do not allow yourself to get stuck in the moment. Do not allow the negative times shape you, but learn from them and use them as stepping stones if need be to move you in a new direction.

Some days it is a constant battle with the voice inside us. We can often be our own biggest critics. Add on what others say to us, and our insecurities grow. We often focus on our flaws rather than building on our gifts. The challenge is to set your focus in the right direction.

While everyone's journey to recovery is different, three things I fall back on are faith, hope, and love. I believe these three ingredients helped fuel my recovery. By focusing on what you have instead of what you have lost, you naturally gravitate toward the positive. If you focus on your loss only, your road to recover will be that much longer. Have faith that you are strong enough to face your loss and get through the pain, allow yourself to hope for new things that will bring you happiness and fulfillment, and, perhaps most importantly, recognize the love you have and the love others have for you. Let your heart, mind, and passion lead the way. Don't waste time on worry, rather keep on pursuing the opportunities that will send you in the right direction. Embracing the change is a huge chunk of your recovery.

Growing up, we always had a family picnic on Sunday afternoon. At the time, I didn't fully appreciate them and the time with family members that produced more laughter and love than anything else. Back then, most stores had limited hours on Sunday, and that really gave people time to bond with each other. Today, with more things to do, more places of business open on Sunday, our time is even more precious. We have a tendency of tuning everyone out these days; we're wrapped up in our own worlds, which we create. Sometimes it's not bad to go back to the basics and focus more on friends and family. It's your time and you have to choose how you want to spend it. I believe it's important to carve out family time, time spent with those you love. This is where memories get made, memories that might be lost if you wait to long to have a gathering. These memories are priceless and are all we have left when we lose the ones we love and the ability to make more memories with them. These times of love and laughter will create the memories that will gain you mileage in your recovery when you need it the most.

At my weekend job in a vineyard, I watch as people gather for showers, birthdays, meetings, or family reunions. I often hear people comment as they are leaving, "We have to do this more often." We do and we should.

I would also tell people what they mean to you. Sometimes it's a simple act that can mean so much. Growing up, I was always training myself to become a professional athlete. That meant eating, and a lot of times I didn't want to.

Gigante's was a family-owned deli in my hometown. It was owned by super nice people and they had the best grinders. I loved their meatball grinder and had a ton of them through the years. It's upsetting to say when I was writing this book in 2020 that the Gigantes decided to sell the business. This was a loss for our town, believe me. In 1989 when I was in the hospital recovering from my car accident, I lost sixty pounds in three weeks. I didn't care for the hospital food and all I could think about was a meatball grinder from Gigante's. My dream came true when the Gigante family sent me down a meatball grinder and a coke. Sometimes it's those little things that mean the most. That started a great relationship between their family and mine. I have a lot to thank this family for, but most of all for showing a young man how to lead with your heart.

Seeing it From the Other Side

"There is nothing that exists that has only one side. Even a piece of paper, thin as it is, has two sides."

—Terry Goodkind

Just as I've said it's important to weed out toxic people from your life, I suggest you also weed out hurtful, harmful pains or thoughts. Not all memories are good ones after all. When my wife passed away in 2005, my in-laws were living with us. After Agnes's death, they continued to live with the kids and myself for a little more than a year. At first it was all about the children and teaching them that love still existed. Out of respect for my wife, I didn't date or see anyone for a year. I had a lot of co-workers and friends stop by to buoy my spirits. When I would laugh or smile, it was tough on my mother-in-law Regina. I suppose she wasn't ready to see me smile. Maybe it somehow lessened, in her eyes, the grief I felt in losing her daughter. It didn't. A moment of happiness does not negate the pain, but it's all in your perspective.

The tension between the two of us began to grow. Communication slowed and what should have been a loving environment began to change. We needed to go in different directions. It wasn't that we didn't love each other; it was just that we were healing differently and we began to focus on things that didn't really matter. We blew petty issues out of proportion. We let our anger smother our heads and hearts. My in-laws moved out and Regina and I didn't speak for a good month.

I've learned, as I got older, to try and put myself in other people's shoes. It never hurts to see a situation from someone else's perspective. Just because we're not wrong, doesn't make us right. My friend Ron Garney taught me this. Often when I call him and give him my side of the story, he will say, "I'm your friend, but . . ." That's when I know I may need to consider something more. When I was going through the situation with my mother-in-law, I told Ron that she and I had both lost daughters and I felt she should be able to relate to this. Ron simply said, "She doesn't know how."

I began to think about and see things through Regina's eyes. She had watched the kids grow up. She was a big part of their lives. I understand, now, as children get older they begin to find their own place in life, but my children were too young at this point for me to understand that. Regina was afraid she would lose the children too, but I never kept my kids from seeing my in-laws. That wasn't even an issue. I thought of my wife when it came to that. If it were me who had passed away, I'd have wanted Agnes to keep my parents in their lives. Certain relatives should always be allowed to be a part of the children's lives, even if a spouse, their connection to the children, has passed away.

Eventually, Regina and I were able to put aside our differences and focus on what was most important—the children. We both loved them, and we both wanted what was best for them.We accepted that no one was right, or wrong; we just saw things differently. I was lucky to have people giving me great advice when I needed it most. To this day, my children have a wonderful relationship with their grandmother, and I believe all are better for it.

My mother was one of those people who always gave me good advice. She pointed out to me that while both my mother-in-law and I had both lost daughters, I had to consider that my daughter didn't have children. She said I had to understand that the children were an extension of Agnes, and .... Soon my mom told me this, I began to notice how my mother-in-law would point out the things in the kids that reminded her of Agnes. I started to understand the other side that I hadn't been seeing. My mother was able to open my eyes and I was able to open my heart. My relationship with Agnes's mother grew so much after this.

This is why it's important to have a good support system around you. My mother tapped into my heartstrings and gave me perspective; my friend Ron gave me the right mindset to make the right decision. Thanks to them my relationship with my children's grandmother was saved and I was able to honor Agnes's memory. I remember my father used to say, "There's your side of the story, there's their side of the story, and somewhere in between is most likely the truth." Sometimes you have to look a little harder for it.

Relationships are not Disposable

"A relationship is like a house. When a light bulb burns out you do not go and buy a new house, you fix the light bulb."

—Anonymous

One of the things I learned from and admired most about my grandparents and their generation was that things are not disposable. Today we take for granted what we have and we throw things away too fast, including relationships. How many times do we throw in the towel because at that moment things aren't going our way? Both sets of my grandparents stood by each other, no matter what the odds or circumstances of their relationships. Nowadays it seems we don't have that tolerance to keep something going.

That being said, there is an argument for getting out of a bad relationship. For example, if a relationship is toxic, if there's cheating or abuse, if you can not find happiness, then you have every right to get out. But if there is a foundation built on love and trust that is currently facing a difficult situation, I believe it is worth fighting for.

History does not always repeat itself and people deserve a chance. Just because a previous partner cheated on you before doesn't mean the next person will. I'm not saying not to use judgment, I'm just saying don't judge someone for someone else's mistake. Relationships are something you have to keep working on. There will be good times and bad. I will always side with working it out rather than tossing it out. I like to focus on the things I fell in love with, not the things that bother me. If you focus on the negative things, the relationship will go downhill fast.

Nobody's perfect, but you could be perfect together. Love is a precious gift. Self-love is important, but love that projects outward can show you an amazing life.

When I was young, my mother always took me to spend time with my grandparents. She would say, "You never know when they'll be gone." It's always something to think about. When we are young, mortality is the last thing on our minds. You think everyone is going to be with you forever. In my first book, I explain how, when I was ten years old, my Grandfather Gannon was being taken to the hospital by ambulance. He made the drivers stop so he could talk to me. He said, "Your grandfather is an asshole. I've smoked and drank and now it's catching up with me."

I'm not a big drinker because of my grandfather's words that day. I didn't go with the flow when my friends started drinking. I made the decision not to drink, smoke, or do drugs. I listened to my grandfather who had been there and done that. My friends and the other kids at school pretty much respected my decision. I was only harassed twice my whole four years of high school. I stood my ground. I was also going after my goal of being a professional athlete and I didn't think those products were conducive to reaching that goal. We all have choices to make, choose wisely.

Visit, Just Don't Unpack

"Just do it better than you did it yesterday."

—Joe Kuczo

I've been told I live in the past. While that's one way you can look at it, I see it more as using my past to face my future with strength and confidence. Using my past experiences to battle through whatever struggle or problem comes my way. I've done it before, I can do it again. I liken it to a house. There are times when our life needs a remodel, an update. You use the foundations of what you built, learn from your mistakes, and create something new and better while still appreciating the framework of where you started.

While I focus more on the better moments in my past than I do the negative, I do revisit those sad experiences every so often. I think it's important to appreciate how far you've come while not wallowing in your past. While you will likely never forget those painful days, you need to find a way to move beyond them.

I have scars, physical and emotional, from different days of my life that have caused me pain and altered my life. Do I look at them and see the pain? Of course, but I have faced my pain, embraced my pain, and then conquered my pain. I took control of my life, set new goals, and discovered the new God-given gifts I never knew I had.

Everyday, somewhere, people talk themselves out of a job, out of recovery, out of a relationship because they don't believe in themselves. This only serves to deny them the opportunity. We've all heard the saying, "You won't know unless you try." Sometimes you have to stick it out through the rough patches.

While physical pain is easy to see, it's right on the surface, you can notice the limp, bruise, or wound, mental pain is harder to detect. It is all too often hidden by a smile, by productivity, simply existing. Just because others can't see your pain does not make it any less real or any less important and painful. Know what you're up against, acknowledge it, and find a way to move past it. Life is too short to be stuck in sorrow. There's a way to get your life back, to move past something that is tearing you up inside, but you have to want it and you have to believe you can do it. It's hard to do the things you don't want to do, most of the time you won't see the rewards of the acts right off the bat. Give yourself a break and take it slow. Celebrate the small accomplishments. Take it one day, one hour, even one minute at a time. You will get through today. Then worry about tomorrow. Don't waste a lifetime on something that can be fixed. Will you make mistakes? Yes. Learn from them and get past them. I've made my share and it hasn't stopped me. We learn, or at least we should try and learn, something new every day. Today is where you turn sorrow and suffering into success.

When I look back on my life, my first memory is of me being burnt by bacon grease in a terrible freak accident when I was very young. I can't say why it happened. Maybe God was preparing me for the tidal wave of tragedies I would face in my lifetime. The pain I experienced at that young age was significant and temporary and I think on some level the experience taught me that I could get through it, no matter how bad it seemed at the time. I was left with significant scars that I also had to work to accept.

One day during my senior year in high school, a teacher asked me if I would change that night of the accident. I said I would change some of the outcomes, that obviously I'd want Marc Izzo back, I wish Matt and I weren't hurt as bad as we were, but as far as what I learned? What I took out of that car mentally? I wouldn't change a thing. When you are knocking on heaven's door, you learn to appreciate life immensely, including the lessons it teaches you. You learn to see what's really important. The little problems don't faze you anymore because you know there are far worse situations out there. I have built up what some would say is a tolerance to certain tragedies. This is not to say I don't care or that I would wish tragedies on anyone, of course I would not. It's just that after what I have experienced, I see things from a different perspective than most. Times of crisis don't control my mindset.

The most important thing you can take away from this book is that I made my share of mistakes too. I've had dark days and bad days, but I was able to recover from them because of the way I conditioned myself. So stop beating yourself up and start beating your demons.

One of my biggest mistakes was when my daughter Danielle died. I didn't let my other children visit or hold her. I thought I was doing the right thing by protecting them. I was wrong. They were stronger than I thought they were. They all said they wanted to meet her, but Agnes and I made the judgment call to keep them from her. I wish I had some advice, but everything and everyone seemed to shut down around me. There are times when you have to make a decision, and right or wrong you have to live with it. With everything I learned after the fact, I would have done it differently, but what is done is done and accepting that is part of the healing. My Uncle Joe used to say, "Just do it better than you did it yesterday." That's all we can do. Mistakes will be made, so learn from them and make a better decision next time.

After a tragedy or a life-changing event, you might have to restart your life. Forgiveness is sometimes the greatest way to go. Leave those harmful, hateful memories in your past and give yourself a pass. Never get used to the pain, recognize it, accept it, and leave it in the past. I've seen people stay in a phase of pain because they became used to it. Some even get stuck in a moment of time. I have not allowed myself to stay in the pain. Throughout the first forty years of my life, something bad happened to me in each decade, but a lot of good happened as well. When I look back, I don't see the pain, I see the pride, the love, the strength and this picks me up.

So how does one do the same? First have faith in yourself, faith that you can accomplish and overcome the task at hand. Start small and appreciate the small accomplishments. For example, say you start going to the gym. After two or three weeks maybe you start to lose focus. Maybe the results are not what you thought they should be. The scale isn't going down as fast as you'd like. Remember, positive changes are going on in your body that you might not even notice. Celebrate every day you make it there. stick with it and take pride with finishing what you set out to do.

Results will be your reward, so don't be quick to quit. Don't manufacture problems or make excuses, let go of the little stuff and keep your eye on your goal. Maybe that goal is to make it to the gym just once a week at first. You can eventually increase it and succeed if you believe in yourself.

Will you have difficult days? Of course. There are going to be things that trigger your emotions. These triggers can sometimes be the key to holding you back. We get stuck in a dark place because we allow things to keep bringing us back there. Triggers could stem from holidays, anniversaries, birthdays, and dates of loss or maybe even a song, a voice, a tone. Try and recognize your triggers. When you find yourself in that bad place, stop and think. What brought you there? What started those feelings, those thoughts? It might be the date, the time, a sound, a smell. You might not recognize it right away, but when you start taking notice, a pattern will likely emerge. If it works for you, start a journal so you can go back and look for that pattern. Talk to a therapist. Find whatever works so you don't allow those triggers to keep bringing you down and sabotaging your recovery. Once you recognize the trigger, you can work to heal from it. Retrain your triggers, find a reason to look past the loss of the day. Stare down the enemy. Stand up for yourself.

As you navigate your recovery, it's important to be patient with yourself. It's a long road. Make a plan and stay on track. Be prepared for things to take a while, most things won't change over night (focus on the small victories). Keep yourself busy and continue to live your life.

In the midst of your grief, pull someone else up. It's a great feeling to be able to help someone else with his or her problems. It can be uplifting for both the person and you. While I think it's easier it is easy to focus on your own pain, I think healing becomes easier when you can help with someone else's healing process. That is not to say you should I am not saying put your own healing on the back burner, definitely not. Continue to be kind to yourself and work on your own healing.

Things can change if you want them to. You can find many ways to replace the hurt with ways to help yourself. While I keep telling you to focus on the positive, I don't want you to ignore the pain. Balance the good with the bad. I sometimes listen to songs that remind me of the people I've lost, and while it brings the pain of the loss back to me, I also think of the love they gave me, I focus on the positive and savor my memories of those people. I found that if I could focus on what they gave me, it made me appreciate what a gift it was to have them in my life. It's not about failure, that's going to happen, keep your mind focused on finding that way to succeed.

Faith

"God whispers to us in our pleasures, speaks in our conscience, but shouts in our pains."

— C.S. Lewis

I wouldn't be where I am without my faith. While I don't push my faith on anyone, I think everyone should give it a try. The Bible has so many stories from which to learn The way I see it? God saved my life and has given me the strength to smile and survive. The night of the car accident, I was in and out of that car many times, not always buckling my seat belt. But, just moments before impact, I put my seatbelt on. Did something tell me to do that? I don't know, but I do know it was one of the reasons I survived. I was also in the front passenger side of that car, the seat referred to as "the death seat" due to . But my seat came off its rudders upon impact and was thrown into the backseat. I was given a second chance. I truly believe I was kept here for a reason, just as I believe God puts people in our lives for reasons we may not ever see or realize. Sometimes they are there to help us, to teach us. Sometimes we help and teach them. Sometimes those lessons are painful, but lessons nonetheless. In the Bible, many stories are about trials that happen to people that have them questioning their faith. Your faith won't save you from pain and loss, but it does help you see your way through it to recovery. If you have faith and trust God (whatever form that god takes) to get you through a difficult situation you will find your peace.. I've had many days where I wanted to question God and ask, "Why are you doing this to me?" But it is not for us to question why. It's for us to ask, "What now?" Only then can you stop playing the blame game and get on with your purpose.

Those who stay in their sorrow and blame the world around them refuse to see the new path or direction God is laying out for them. In a strange way, the more bad things that happened to me, the more my faith increased. I've God has allowed me to overcome many adversities. In an interview with a local television station, I was asked if I ever thought of myself as Job from the Bible. I see how you can make that comparison. Job and I have faced difficulties in different times in our lives. I was raised to believe in God and I had great examples around me. I was never pushed into the faith, it just always felt right. You have to find what works for you, and that may mean trying a few different things. You'll know it when you find it, but you have to look. God is all around us, but he's subtle. In 2019, I was working at my dispatch job and I received a call from a father who had just lost his adult son in a tragic car accident. He wanted to know if any of his son's belongings were still in the car. My boss told me that the car was covered in blood, but he would check again. Come to find out, that there was a sweatshirt hanging in the back of the car without a stain on it. This sweatshirt was the last gift the man had bought for his daughter. The man's father was able to give that gift to his granddaughter. Think of how meaningful that sweatshirt is to that daughter now. How do you explain that? Stories and moments like these, to me, prove there's something greater out there.

I call on my faith every day. I pray because I certainly don't have this life figured out, at all. My faith propels me into the next day and I believe it will heal me from and for the next challenge. The Bible, for me, has a tip or solution for any problem. I read and learn from the stories I read there. Whatever your belief, look to your faith for the answers. I believe we are presented with problems in our lives for a reason. I look back and see how many lives I've been able to touch because of what I've seen and experienced in my life.

I do know there is a difference between belief and commitment. My friend Matt showed me that. There's a phrase in the bible that says, "This too shall pass away." . It basically means that bad things will pass and you will survive. Sometimes we need help, our faith can help us carry our burdens, whether that faith be in the form of prayer or in the form of a good friend you can lean on. My friend Matt Escoto always worked everyday to get closer to Jesus Christ. He made a commitment to Christ. Sometimes our faith may seem to forsake us though. Why do we need to lose someone we love? What kind of God does this to us? I believe that when God chooses not to answer a prayer and change a painful situation, he gives you the strength to get through. Is it fair to blame God when he doesn't answer one of our prayers? Consider this. A gentleman I used to work with told me a story about how he was hooked on drugs. He couldn't see himself beating this addiction on his own. He told me that one night he dropped to his knees and asked God for help. He said he surrendered his life to Christ. By the end of the week he was completely free of drugs and never went back to them. Did God have a hand in this? That's up to you to decide what to believe, but I think it's fair to say that this man's faith was a definite force, whether it was faith in himself or a greater spiritual being.

If you are at this moment of suffering and pain and feel as if you can't do any more, I encourage you to seek help. Whether from a professional or a family member or a friend. Talk to someone and above all, have faith. Have faith in yourself, in your worth, and in your ability to make a difference and have a purpose. I've witnessed and heard stories of faith making the difference too many times to discount them. You have so many precious gifts in your life, see them, appreciate them, live for them.

Please understand God's love is beyond anything we can measure. It's important to allow people to almost feel God's love through ourselves. The people today need to see it and or feel it. God gives you peace to bear the pain. We are also given the chance of an afterlife due to one man's sacrifice.

Learn from the Past

"Those who do not learn history are doomed to repeat it".
—George Santayana

There is a point in life when we need to push and not pull. A time when you need to start pushing away the blame or excuses rather than pulling all those negative things toward you. I haven't always been positive about certain things in my life. For example, I thought love wouldn't come my way again. I had it in my mind that I had had something special and it wouldn't be fair of me to ask for it again.

When my mother was in the hospital battling end-stage cancer, I didn't have better things to don't worry about, I didn't sit around thinking of what I could say to her or do for her, I was just there. If I could warm her heart just for a moment, I could ease her pain for that moment.

The day my mother passed away, my sisters Mo, Maryanne, and Jessica and I were holding her hands. We all held onto her last breath. I found out at that moment, it didn't matter our age, it just all hit us, maybe in different ways, but at the moment it sure looked the same. Age doesn't prepare you for pain. Pain prepares you for pain. Even with that being said, I was the one who had seen the most loss at this point. The immediate loss brought us to the same place, but how we all healed was up to us. I want to say for most of us it opened our hearts and eyes. A new world starts after any loss, but what that world will now consist of relies on us.

I could bring you a moment. You could bring me a moment. There needs to be more moments. The moments in our lives are what add up and bring us joy, even after they are gone. Begin to find and appreciate your moments, the ones you are given as well as the ones you can give. It's important to see the world outside the circumstances you are in. How are you functioning as an individual? Are the things in your head overwhelming what the world is offering you? Are you shaping you, or is life shaping you? Read that again. Are you shaping life, or is life shaping you? Are you appreciating the moments, or are they passing you by?

If your surroundings are shaping or influencing your life, then how can you change your circumstances? It could be your physical location, the friends you are keeping, the job you have. Maybe it's the house you are in that keeps you in the past, brings you to that hard or dark place in your life. Maybe maybe you don't have the money or the means to move out of the house, but that doesn't mean you are stuck. When my wife passed away I didn't allow my mind to stay in the memories of what we had. I looked at our house as something we had built together. Everything we built together was now up to me. Instead of staying wrapped in negative thoughts (her not being there to see the finish), I took pride in what we accomplished. Years later when I moved into my parent's house where my father had died, I didn't focus on that terrible memory. I focused on how my parents built that house and the great times our family had in it. If you focus on the bad times, that's what you'll end up with. If you are stuck in a house that continues to remind you of a bad situation, remodel. Do a room, a wall at a time. A fresh coat of paint can make a huge difference.

Writer and philosopher George Santayana said, "Those who do not learn history are doomed to repeat it." When you can , learn from your past and build your future, then you are shaping your life, not the other way around. Don't be a prisoner of unresolved issues from your past. It's not about what has happened to you, but rather how you respond to it.

We all have or will face problems at some point in our lives, how you react to those problems determines your course in life. I try to treat people like I would want to be treated. I was even told by my last two employers that I'm too nice. I guess that's a bad thing? If I'm having a bad day, I don't take it out on anyone else. If someone else is having a bad day, I give them space and understanding. Having a bad day is one thing, though, and being an unkind person is completely another. Some people just don't like themselves, and that's the difference from just a bad phase in your life. We all can tell the difference from a bad day and someone's nasty core. This is where you need to decide if you're going to push or pull. We can't always choose our co-workers and we certainly can't choose our family, but we can choose to stay or go. People who don't like themselves will always find something wrong with others, being on the receiving end of that can be very damaging.

Our thoughts are very influenced. We become what we think we'll be. If you stay around a person who is always finding fault with you, you might start believing them, and this can be detrimental to your recovery, which is all about making steady progress toward the positive..

I have often relied on examples I had around me. All my mentors have suffered in some way at some time, that's why they became my mentors. I admired how they overcame and moved forward. They didn't allow their circumstances to overtake them. They pushed the negative away and pulled the positive to them. As they did, you and I will have days or moments when we'll slip, and that's okay. It's part of the process. Don't lose sight of your goals, never let them slip out of reach, keep them close and conquer the challenge. Don't harbor bitterness in your heart, head, or soul. See yourself as being tempered by the trials and tribulations and ready yourself for the next battle.

Focus on the Future

Children are the living messages we send to a time we will not see.
                                                    —John F. Kennedy

I have three amazing children, Billy Jr., Jeremy, and Casey. All three have seen their share of heartbreak and loss. Each has risen above the situations they've been dealt and look for more out of their lives. First and foremost, they're good people and are willing to help others. I can't even count the amount of times someone has told me that my children have helped them without being asked.

Billy is now twenty-six and lives in my grandparents' house. He is remodeling it in a way that would have made Grandpa Gannon so proud. Five generations of my family have lived in the house he built.

I sometimes think of what was and what can be. Watching my children achieve their goals is the greatest gift a parent can receive. I admit I miss the younger years, so to the young parents out there, I say, don't rush them, that time will come quick enough." Take pride and joy in building a bond with your children. Throw that ball with them, see that movie, bring them to a show, take the vacation.

My wife Agnes used to read a book or do homework with the children every night. She believed in tradition and wanted to pass it along to our children. Growing up in a family of different cultures, our children are the best of both of us. They were all blessed with my father's athletic abilities, able to walk onto any sports field and just play. They are all blessed with their mother's brain and lust to learn. I'm proud to say that all three of my children have taken advantage of every opportunity given to them. They've always made the most out of everything that came their way, good or bad.

Agnes and I had high hopes and high expectations for all my children and they have exceeded my imagination. My children are great examples in not just what they've overcome but how they've learned to help others. They are a true blessing to me. When Agnes was at her lowest stage, I was able to get her to see what we both had in front of us with them. Again, that's another example of seeing what we have and not focusing on what we've lost.

Author Bill Gannon's son Billy, Jr. (left) with his mother Maryann and son Jeremy and daughter Casey in 2010.

The bitterest tears shed over graves are for words left unsaid and deeds left undone.

—Harriet Beecher Stowe

A bad day only lasts for twenty-four hours. Why let it stretch to weeks, months, or even years? How long should the darkness cover your heart? The answer to that question is different for everyone. For some it might take a little longer to ride out the storm, and that's okay. Be patient with yourself.

People often approach me at my speaking engagements. They want to share and compare stories, and some share regrets as well. The regret I hear the most involves feelings over a disagreement between them and their lost loved one. They often feel guilty about how their relationship ended, that amends were not made. Keep that in mind when you argue with family and friends. Take a moment and think about what is at stake. Is it worth the pain you are causing to keep the feud going. Hurtful words and sentiments can be taken back and apologized for, time lost will never be recovered. Giving someone a second chance now may erase the pain later, even if the reunion is unsuccessful at least you did your best to make amends. Should something happen at this point, you should be able to have a quicker recovery because of your efforts.

Sometimes people want to go their own path in life, and there are times when there are no happy reunions. Unfortunately, sometimes there are no happy endings. If you were unsuccessful in making amends, you can't beat yourself up about it. Learn to leave those people behind. Not everyone wants to be saved, as sad as that may be, but that is not on you. Be bigger and better than the other person or situation. Bitterness comes from many different angles. Some get mad from what happened, some get mad at what didn't happen, and some get mad at both. Get beyond the bitterness, it's not worth the energy it takes. Don't allow your life to go down that path. Bitterness can consume all aspects of your life in a negative way. It keeps you focused on what you don't have, rather than seeing what you do have. After a tragedy, it's so important to keep seeing what gifts you still have.

One way to stave off the bitterness is to make time in your day to better yourself. You can read, exercise, or maybe just have a good meal. See the blessing outweigh the bitterness. Really see it and appreciate it, no matter how small a blessing it is. You will enjoy life much more. It's hard for bitterness to creep into a heart that is full of love and gratitude. Surround yourself with people who lift you up, not bring you down. Find the people who complete you.

I'm just a simple guy who has his master's degree from the school of hard knocks. Just as anyone who walks this earth, I'm learning every day. I didn't choose all these battles in my life, they were sent my way and I was forced to deal with them. They, in turn, have taught me valuable lessons, which I hope to pass on to you. Failures happen to us all and know that the greatest tragedy isn't the falling down, it's the not getting back up. You have a life left to live, start seeing that life in a positive way, focus on the things you still have that are really important. Take that day off to reconnect with someone, or just take it off to take care of you. Whatever you need to further your recovery is not too much to ask. You are worth the work.

I can tell you, it's a lot easier to learn by listening, than by learning the hard way. Never allow too much time to go by. Make time before time takes something from you.

This book has a lot of stories about life lessons, some are everyday simple ones and others are on a grander scale. My sophomore English teacher, the late Lisa Toman, turned my academic career around. I was taking her midterm exam, one third of which was based on vocabulary. I was making what could be called a cheat sheet. My desk was a mere two feet from hers. She said, "You are sitting too close to think you'll get away with that."

I replied, " I'll hand it to you when we start."

"Yes you will',' she quickly replied.

I handed her my cheat sheet and the exam started. I went right to that section of the exam and finished it rather quickly. She asked if she could correct that section since I was already finished. She took that section and didn't bother me until the exam was over. She collected the exams from everyone in the class as the bell rang. I stayed and asked her how I did.

"As far as the vocabulary goes," she said, "you got ninety-nine out of one hundred."

I was happy and said, "There's not much room for improvement there."

"Your vocabulary is fine," she said. "But you, on the other hand, have plenty of room for improvement."

She told me I was cheating myself in the classroom and she was right. She didn't call me out in front of the class, she did it in private, just the two of us, and that in itself was a lesson as well. See, it was not about addressing my faults in front of others and having all eyes on me, rather this wise woman wanted me to look inside myself. She made me see that I was cheating myself by being lazy. For the rest of the year she encouraged me to try my best. She didn't allow me to hold myself back. She said she was going to hold me to a higher standard until I learned to do it myself. I was lucky to have such an amazing teacher in my life. She pushed me toward a better me.

Find A New Focus

"All the art of living lies in a fine mingling of letting go and holding on."
— Henry Havelock Ellis

Sometimes we need to find a new focus or fall back on an old comfortable one in order to make our lives fulfilled. The loss of my daughter brought me to the lowest point in my life. There was not a lot to cling to in the days following her death. People don't really know what to say about the loss of a child, and I don't blame them. You hear time after time "There's nothing worse" or "I can't even imagine." Even the always-positive person I considered myself to be was reduced to tears for forty-eight hours.

It was my son Billy who pulled me from the depths of Hell. One day, about two days after my daughter's death, I had taken my children, Billy, Jeremy, and Casey, along with a few of their cousins to play miniature golf to try and lighten the day. I was still struggling, and about halfway to the complex those uncontrollable tears came over me. The smiles on the kids' faces left as the car's atmosphere changed. Billy spoke up, in the way children do, and said, "Hey Dad, when are you going to have fun again?" As I worked to gather myself, I thought about those young lives I was affecting. The feeling of being on a downward spiral began to lift as I began to realize that I had a life left to live, a job left to do, a purpose greater than my own. By no means was I 100 percent back to where I was, but I certainly was no longer losing ground. My focus shifted from my own pain to helping my children with theirs. I didn't stop feeling the pain, but now I knew I needed to become more than the pain. My family was looking for me to show them the way out.

If you focus on the negative, what do you think is going to come out of that? As I was working my way back to play football after the accident, I clung to anything positive. I was surrounded by doubt and disbelief. My body was betraying me as much as harsh words were. I knew I faced an uphill battle, but I was prepared to battle. I began focusing on what I could do, not what I could not. I worked on strengthening the parts of my body and mind that were weak, one step at a time. If my mind or body went in a direction I didn't want them to, I worked on focusing on something else, something positive. If I couldn't run as fast as I once did, I had to sharpen my mind to make quicker decisions and work on a quicker release of the ball. I found a new focus, I adapted. Adapting was a huge part of my recovery. It was about finding a way to make me the best I could be with what I had.

My advice to you is to take stock of what you have. Use all of the tools you have. We should not ever waste our gifts. Prepare yourself for the good path with a different outlook, or just a new understanding on how you perceive things. When my son Billy called me out for being and staying sad, he gave me a tool for my arsenal. I knew I had to be there for my other children, the children who remained. I had to be there for my family, to show them the way forward. Thankfully, I had amazing people around me to show *me* the way. I followed their example to set the example for my own family.

Do you have those people in your life? Think about it, you must have someone you can look up to. Seek out that person whose life view is almost larger than life. The people who are bigger than most of their daily problems. There are examples all over the place, right there ready to inspire us.

Surround yourself with the right people and put yourself in the right mindset. Do this and you will get better faster. That is what it is all about. You need to find that happy ground again. Find that place where you can be comfortable again and enjoy the life you have left to live. Do not waste time in pity. Pity gets you nowhere.

I loved the game of football, but after the accident, I had to accept that I would never play the game again. I did coach for a while and learned to give back, but I could no longer physically play. I had to find a new way to appreciate the sport and begin to find a life off the field. Don't pity yourself for what you have lost, realize that God gives us more than one gift to work with. It is on us to follow our hearts and develop these gifts. Find your floatation device, the thing that keeps your head above water and stops you from drowning. There may be a time when you don't feel like you have the strength to swim, so hold on to that thing, whatever it is at the time. Even if you are simply floating, look for that rescue boat in the distance, believe they are coming, that better days are ahead, and you can hang on. Keep your eye on the prize.

Sometimes in life we overcomplicate things, overthink things. I found it helpful to focus on the basics. If you're sad, look for happiness. Heartache can be defeated by love and laughter, but sometimes we don't seek it when we need it most. We allow our grief to take the wheel. Heartache, grief, anger, they will all happen and maybe it will take the wheel at some point, but never hand them the keys. You have a life left to live. What do you want to do with your remaining days? Some people make a bucket list. They make goals or take trips to find themselves again or to just to live a little. Even if your goals are lofty ones. at least you gave it a try. As long as you keep climbing the mountain you'll earn respect, especially self-respect.

I met a gentleman recently, his name is Paul. Paul and I both were involved in car accidents when we were seventeen years old. We sustained a lot of the same injuries that we had to overcome. I've had a bit more time in this area, however. Paul was only twenty when I met him and was still using a cane; he was still finding his new normal. He asked me to help him carry some picture frames to his car for him. He said, "You move pretty well," and said that gave him hope in getting better. He then explained how he had wasted three years being bitter before he found art, which gave him a new purpose and became a new driving force in his life. Let this serve as another reminder that we are all here for a reason, just sometimes that reason changes and we need to find it.

One particularly beautiful day I was at a family picnic speaking with my sister Maryann and my brother-in-law's brother Rob. Rob was talking about how he would love to do more good deeds, but just doesn't have enough time. Rob is a great guy and really would give you the shirt off his back, but at the time he was putting his three kids through college. His time and resources were running low . As we continued to talk my sister and I pointed out how Rob had raised his children to become polite, productive people in society. That was his purpose at that time in his life, and that deed, that accomplishment would have its own effect on the world. Sometimes it's more about the ripple effect than what is immediately at hand. A ripple effect is a situation in which, like the ripples expanding across the water when an object is dropped into it, an effect from an initial state can be followed outward incrementally. Raising good children is, in essence, the ripple effect of life. Two good people create a family of good people. If we instill in our children a good moral compass, then we've made a difference in this life.

These little things can have so much more meaning if we stop and appreciate them. Being an influence to the people around us, making the most out of our relationships,teaching our kids to take care of and think for themselves, etc. Focus on these things as you find your way to recovery.

It's Okay to Be Okay

"Guilt is to the spirit what pain is to the body."

—Elder David A. Bednar

Survivor's guilt is a common consequence of tragedy. You ask yourself why you were the one given another chance. This guilt can weigh on you. You could spend a lifetime wondering why. I explain in *To Lose But Not Fail* that my third-grade catechism teacher, Mrs. Lewis, seemed to always appear in my path after one of my challenges. She would say, "God kept you here for a reason." I have never questioned her wisdom but didn't really appreciate it until after the accident. It wasn't long after the car accident that I received a sign that maybe I *was* here for a reason, and maybe it was more than just to play football.

It was a Saturday in July. I had had a really bad day trying to work out; nothing was going right for me. At this point I was making huge strides and hoping to get back to the football field for my senior year. At about 1:00 in the afternoon, I decided to call it a day. I took and shower and called my friend to see if she wanted to go see *Karate Kid 3* with me It took her a long time to answer the phone and when she did, she sounded out of breath.At first she didn't jump at my invitation, but I kept pushing her. She finally agreed and I headed over to pick her up for the 5:00 p.m. show. I didn't notice anything different when I saw her and we enjoyed the movie. We then headed out to play mini-golf, both of us being competitive as ever. We bet dinner on the game. I am far from the best mini-golfer, so I ended up buying. After we got our food, we got into a deep conversation. We started talking about life. I was talking about how fragile it was and how precious every moment was. That's when her tears began to fall.

She told me she had been planning on committing suicide earlier that day. She had the car started in the garage, written a goodbye letter to her family, and had been ready to go through with it when the phone rang, and rang, and rang. She felt like that was a sign from her angel pulling her back from the darkness. It was at this moment that I knew I was still here for a reason.

We talked about how many things she had going for her. She asked if I had those thoughts, and I told her I didn't. I wasn't afraid to die, but I certainly didn't want to rush it. As our conversation continued, we turned the tears into laughter. She saw her strengths again and lost those dark feelings. She saw her worth again. We talked a lot over the next few weeks, but never mentioned anything about that moment of darkness. Odd thing is, that day was just as important to me as it was to her. We are still friends to this day and I couldn't imagine life without her. With my football career still up in the air at this point, it was pivotal for me to see and understand that I was here for something other than football. While football certainly was my focus at the time, I learned to broaden my horizon. I saw a new direction for my life.

It's amazing how God works. Sometimes it's as simple as finding a new focus. Regardless of what the loss is, it's best to gather yourself and work with what's left.

I mentioned before that losing my daughter Danielle was the hardest thing I ever had to survive, but I had to turn my grief into strength when I realized my family needed me to restore us to a place without the overwhelming pain. The pain didn't go away, it just was no longer my first focus. I kept busy because being busy keeps you going in the right direction. I know some will say that being busy keeps you from facing your fears, facing your pain, but I look at it as not giving into those fears or pains. Be the warden of your own prison and give yourself a pardon. Don't settle into that survivor mode. Find that new purpose when the firsts are over. Allow yourself to visit the pain when an important day comes up in the first year after a loss. Maybe it's the first Christmas, or birthday, or anniversary without your loved one, acknowledge the pain, but don't let it lead you off the ledge. Find something that makes a difference in your day, or in someone else's day. Find the happy. Turn the missing into meaning.

When I think of the people who influenced me, I see how they worked to bounce back from their losses. They were able to put their pain aside and help push me in the right direction. Agony will keep you in one place, while love will lead you in a new direction. As the distance grows from the negative memories, you'll see your life restore itself. Take a moment now and think of someone you know who has defied the odds. Put yourself in that hope mode. What would you say to a friend or loved one if you saw them suffering through something and you want to help them to bounce back. If necessary look at yourself in the mirror and give yourself that needed pep talk to get you moving forward.

We all rally around people when a tragedy strikes, and that's fine, however it's after the first six weeks and the dust settles that that person could probably really use support. A simple call, text, or card can make the biggest difference. It's easy to let someone know how important he or she is. During my struggles, my Uncle Joe Kuzzo would always send me inspirational quotes to keep me moving forward.

It's important to share your stories and experiences with people because you never know when or who they might help. It may even help in ways you didn't foresee; there are things that I've done in sports or therapy that could inspire someone in the business world, you just never know.

You should set goals for every aspect of your life, career, family, health, or love. Set some goals and work to achieve them. There are times we might be too ambitious with goals and we're not on schedule with them, and most of the time that's okay. Remember it's you against you and you can win this. The most important thing in this situation is to stay focused and positive. Give yourself credit where credit is due.

Another important tool I used is to have some alone time with God. I loved taking in a view or gazing at the stars. Prayer was important to me. If you don't believe in God, that's your choice, but at least believe in you. Give yourself some downtime, meditate if that's your thing, take a hot bath, whatever relaxes you.

Take some time and figure out what really matters in your life. I loved the game of football, but after the accident it dropped on my priorities list. There are times when you have to make some changes. My father used to tell me, "The older you get, the smarter I'll be." He was right. As we mature, our priorities in life change, tragedy or not. I've been completely blessed by the family and friends I've had around me. That's a major part of the formula for success. Find people who are for you and not just with you and build a support team.

About ten years after my father died, I learned that he had given his varsity letters away to a friend who never was able to earn them by himself. I'm against just giving trophies to teams who don't deserve them, however if someone gave his all and couldn't achieve his goal, that I could live with.

We are all here for certain reasons. I talk about my friend Ron Garney many times in both my books. Ron is an artist in every form of the word. He can act; write songs, sing, and draw. I'm in envy over the talent he has. I would love to be able to do the same things he could do, but I'm not jealous of him, just love his drive and gifts. Enjoy others talents and don't hate them for them.

My friend Dennis Mannion would consistently say life's not fair. When you realize the truth of that, you have a tendency to not sulk over issues but to meet them head on. It's inevitable that life will traumatize us all at some point and when it does, it's important to remember that it's not what happens *to* us, but rather how we handle it. There's something out there that can help you get past your pain. Someone or something will put it in front of you eventually. It's up to you to take it from there.

Some people are just fine with the path of least resistance. They are fine with the easy life. I believe that this isn't a bad way to live as long as you are able to keep the toxic environment out of your life. I know people who find reasons not to go to work because of a coworker. Speed bumps can slow you down, but they shouldn't end your journey. The way I see it, if you never challenge yourself, you will have a more difficult time with life when it shows its ugly side. I suggest not getting stuck in patterns. Don't waste time trying to defend yourself. The older we get, the easier it is to see that we will never please everyone. Some people would love to push you down and keep you there. I believe that by taking the high road, your actions will speak for themselves. Don't spend time worrying about words, they will only hurt you if you let them. It is up to you if you want to waste time worrying about petty things, but I suggest looking past it or maybe using it positively to further your purpose. If you can avoid all the pitfalls associated with letting insults affect you negatively, you will benefit in the long run. I just hope you can find the courage when life calls you to have it. The less you give in your life, the less you can ask for. We live in a negative world now and it is easy to fall into that pattern. I believe we should give all we can. With every gift I give, I discover new things in my life. If you live this way, you need to accept things the way they are.

We are going for It

"I firmly believe that respect is a lot more important, and a lot greater, than popularity."

—Julius Erving

My father was big on respect, he believed it had to be earned. "Respect will take you farther than any trophy or award ever will," he told me. When I was a freshman in high school, this one boy would challenge me all the time. Not to fight him, but to beat him in sports. We never played the same positions, but for three years we verbally sparred with each other back and forth. Our senior year we were on the same football team. This was the same time I was making my comeback from the car accident and he was actually being pretty decent and kept his negative barbs to himself. In the second to last game of the year, a game that would turn out to be my last, I was in the huddle. We were losing the game and the play would mean nothing to anyone but us. The coaches called for a short pass; a quick pitch and catch and end on a positive play. We just happened to disagree. My friend George, who was a spark plug full of heart, looked at me and said, "We are going for it." Without hesitation, I agreed. George gave me thumbs up and when the ball was snapped he went deep. The opposing team was ready for the deep ball and it was intercepted. The game was over. There would be no storybook last throw. I didn't regret the choice, but I just stood there, taking in the moment. I listened to people cheering and knew it was for more than a scoreboard. That's the part that was so special. Those people were rooting for me. They had believed I could do something pretty close to impossible. Some people would view what we did as a failure, but that play, taking that chance to go for it, was the way I wanted to go out. As I stood there, who do you think was the first person to come up to me? After three years of going back and forth and challenging me constantly, he came up to me and said, "Keep that chin up, you have a lot to be proud of." It was at that moment I realized I may not have won the game but I had won the hearts of a lot of people. The game of football had once again taught me something. It was the last time I would step on the field as a player.

When it comes to respect, my father was right, and the most important respect is self-respect. I was able to leave that field that night with no regrets. I will always miss suiting up with those guys, but win or lose we had fun and made the most of it.

Sometimes it helps to see failure as a friend, as a stepping-stone. Life produces failures every day; some are small and nobody notices them, but we most certainly learn from them, so why not apply this to the larger failures in life? We have a tendency to fear failure and that fear will keep you down if you allow it to.

One of those goosebump moments for me came on Thanksgiving of 1988. My dad and I were on our way to my high school for the cross-town rival game when my father said, "You can't be afraid to lose the game." It was his way of telling me to play my game and let the cards fall where they may, but I had practiced so hard to get where I was that I felt taking myself out of the game would be a Cardinal sin. What I didn't realize then was that sometimes we need to have more faith in ourselves.

This was the last game of my junior year and the words of my Uncle Joe were in my mind. He would say, "Inspire your teammates with your words and actions." My Uncle Joe taught me that it wasn't just about making myself better, but it was about showing my teammates and others around me how important *they* were as well.

It's all about working with and relying on your support system, whether that be your family in a tragedy, your friends in a crisis, or your team in an important game. They can lean on you if needed and you can lean on them. You each learn from each other and grow through the experience. Each stage should bring new growth within you; each heartbeat brings you closer to a better your way of life.

We all have things we can do that cannot only help our own lives but others too. Stop feeding into the failure. Always look to gain ground and if you're having a bad day, and you will, don't feed into those days. Draw that line in the sand, grieve if you need to, face your losses and setback, but stand your ground. You may not gain ground that day, but don't allow yourself to lose ground either.

Overcome the opposition in your life, regardless of what it is. Was I shaped by the tragedies? Yes I was, but I kept my hand in the process of the remodel. Life changes, and sometimes it changes often. Find your new territory and flourish in it.

Playing the game for the love of it

There Is Life Left to Live

"You can get busy living, or you can get busy dying."
—Andy Dufresne (played by Tim Robbins), *The Shawshank Redemption*

I love speaking to people on how to overcome the odds in their lives. It could be at a business, a school, a library, or even in a locker room before that big game. I always love hearing from people at the end of my presentation that my story meant a lot to them. I'm always trying to find new ways to cope with pain and loss. It's important to me to keep learning and to pass what I've learned on to others. It's what has helped me heal.

Success is not always the best measure of happiness. I have friends who sing and have never had a number-one hit, but they have a great following and enjoy doing what they are doing. Life is what you make out of it. You have to find your happy and be patient with yourself while doing it. We are not promised a new day, but each day we wake up, we are blessed with one. I woke up on the day after my accident seeing life through new eyes. It was a whole new perspective for me.

I remember speaking to a gentleman a little more than a week after he had lost his son. I wondered, was it too early to talk to him? You can never say when the dust will settle, it's different for everyone. In the beginning, it can be very overwhelming. You are wrapped up in funeral proceedings, friends and family are checking in, a lot. It can feel almost surreal as your brain works to comprehend what has happened. It can feel like a nightmare from which you want to wake and go back to life the way it was, the way you were used to. The truth is that troubles spill into our lives and it's not often we are prepared for them. How we deal with them is up to us. We all heal in our own time, but the sooner we embrace the healing process, the sooner I believe we can find happiness again.

This gentleman's son had passed away soon after he graduated while my daughter never had the chance to take a breath on this earth. He asked if I thought I had it easier because I had been less invested in my child. While it's true I didn't have much time with my daughter, I explained to him that as I held her lifeless body in my arms I thought of all the times I wouldn't get to share with her. I was cheated of all those times he had been gifted with his son. He had memories of milestones to hold on to while I had none. It's a point of view on how you want to see it.

Loss is loss, regardless of what the circumstances are. I was hoping to show this man how to overcome his obstacle no matter how great he thought it was. I wanted to give him new perspective. When we are in the bottom of a hole, we imagine ourselves deeper than we really are. Climbing out can seem an impossible task. Loss is heartbreaking and can bring anyone to his or her lowest point in life. I didn't explain my story to compare it to his, but rather to show him that there is always another way of looking at things and that a new perspective can offer a light at the end of the tunnel.

Life will go on. Will it ever be the same as it was? No, it will never be the same, but the change shouldn't ruin the life you have left to live. You can get busy living, or you can get busy dying. I understand it's not exactly that simple, but it's up to you to make that move to more. You could be that example on how you handle a situation that inspires someone else. In my case it was my children and my wife before she passed away. I worked to be their example. They were my inspiration. Now you need to find something to fight for! It could be your children, your family, or your job; maybe it's all of the above or maybe it's none of the above, maybe it's just you. You are worth fighting for. Find that thing to grab onto so it allows you to pull yourself out of the hole you're in.

What you do today might just determine your future. For example, if you build a loving relationship with someone, yes it will hurt if you lose them, but the loving memories of the time you had will stay in your heart and mind for a lifetime. Remember the real gifts are the time you spent together, and no one can take that away from you. There is always a reason we are still here. We can be that positive example for others or we can settle for less.

I can't say enough about my upbringing. I was fortunate to have a tight-knit, loving family who supported me as I grew up. I fear we have lost the idea of family in today's world. When a sentence or thought always starts with *I* or *me* and not *us* or *we,* that's a major problem in the making. We are all here on this earth to help each other, and very few things should come between the bonds of family.

While the demands of today's society often calls for both parents to work outside the home to make ends meet, families have found a way to make the family unit work. That bond is so important. In my times of loss, it was literally life-saving. My children were the reason I was able to reconnect with life, no matter what was sent my way.

I was releasing a car at work. The gentleman and I were walking to the garage. He was telling me that two boys caused a seven-car collision, then took off. As I opened the garage door we both looked at the vehicle, my first response was, "You were a lucky man." The car had rolled over two times and almost went off the bridge, which would have surely been a fatal fall. As he walked around the now twisted heap of metal, he explained that he was extremely thankful that he had been alone in the car and that one of the first things he did was text his wife a picture of the car on its roof and told her he was okay. He then looked at me and said, "I was blessed to get out of the car with only a shoulder injury."

That man saw what was important in life. I believe there are people in our lives who share their stories with us so that we hopefully see what we truly have. A woman I work with who has seen her share of loss, writes down three things every day that she is thankful for. Positive things happen every day all around us and it's our responsibility to see them. When you suffer a loss, this lesson is so important. Seek and see what remains in your life, that is what is important. Mourn what you have lost, but cherish what you have left.

Is everyone ready and able to do this? No, not by a long shot. I remember another car I worked on. Every part of this car was crushed, except the driver's side cabin. If anyone else had been in this car at the time of the accident, they would have surely been killed. When the young owner of this car arrived to sign the papers, I told him how lucky he was, but he was only concerned about the damage done to his car. He had walked away from the accident without a scratch, so he really didn't experience a tragedy or a loss. While I don't wish harm on anyone, when I see a car in that shape and see the driver not thankful for surviving and having another chance at life, I don't know, I just think there was a major lesson that he didn't see at all.

As we go about our daily lives, we don't realize the effect our actions can and do have on others. I remember being on vacation with my in-laws. My brother-in-law, Jeff Dzierlatka, was praying by the side of his bed before he retired for the night. It's those examples all around us. My brother-in-law, John Roche, dotes on his children, showing everyone a true example of what a father should be. I always said if I could be half of the father he is, I would be happy. When she was younger and our Grandmother Gannon was alive, my sister Mo would finish her job for the day, go home and feed her family, then go take care of our grandmother, showing us all what unconditional love looks like. My best friend, Joe Kurcaba, shows me year after year the meaning of friendship with his unwavering support and understanding. Time and time again people close to me show me how beautiful this life can be. I was young when God opened my eyes to what is important in life. Too often we see someone's flaws before we take the time to see the good in them. I do it myself, but I make a conscious effort not to. Honestly, even if we see the bad in some people, that's up to God to sort out. I know it's easier said than done, but try your best next time to focus on some piece of good rather than react to the bad.

Don't Limit Yourself

Today is the day you can defy the odds.

Too often we are our own worst enemies. We are the ones who keep ourselves from achieving our goals. We put a limit on our own abilities. It is the job of a coach to put the best team on the playing field. In the corporate world, it is the boss who chooses his team, picking those who will best run his business. As the boss and coach of ourselves, we need to recognize and evaluate what skills we possess. We all have a purpose on this earth. We all have God-given gifts that are second nature to us. These gifts are skills we do not have to develop, as they come natural to us. Take advantage of these.

It is important to set goals. Regardless of how lofty the goals might be, strive for them. Never be afraid of adversity, it builds strength. My Uncle Joe Kuczo was head trainer for the Washington Redskins for many years. When I was younger, my goal was to become a professional quarterback. He and I exchanged weekly calls in pursuit of my dream. He made it very clear from the start that it would not be easy but always said it was far from impossible. The advice I received from him was priceless. He repeated time after time that I just needed to find that right combination. I needed to make sure my grades were good enough to get me into a school and that my workouts were sharpening my skills and always making me better. Sometimes when we see our heroes or role models, we think that their level of success is not obtainable to us. While that may be true, it's a goal to work toward. Uncle Joe gave me that right combination of working on both my strengths and weaknesses. It kept me from being frustrated, yet it allowed me to focus on the things I struggled with. If I strayed from the program or fell short of a goal, Uncle Joe would say, "Focus on the lesson." He would tell me to find out where and why I failed and to learn from that. Sometimes our greatest lessons come from failure. By continuing to challenge yourself, you will improve much quicker. It is nice having someone like my uncle to help keep your chin up, giving you that lift when others are not.

We should all have that someone who instills that confidence in us. Doubt is a powerful deterrent. You cannot gain experience through hesitation, but you can gain experience through failure. We need to break our own boundaries and stop placing restrictions on ourselves.

For example, a good personal trainer in the gym is not going to give his clients all the same workout. He will figure out the best combination and formulate that works for each. People are built differently and have different abilities. It is on him, just as it is on you, to identify strengths and witnesses and the best way to work on those. Everyone has to find their own path to success and/or recovery. What works for you, may not necessarily work for someone else and vice versa. It's all in finding that right combination. You will try different things and there will be trial and error, but remember, you can learn as much from failure as you can from success. The road to recovery is not always an easy one, but it is yours to accomplish or not. Believing in yourself is an important first step. Then continue building that belief beyond what you considered possible. When a bad or horrific situation happens, you will most likely find support from friends and family. Take what you need, but do not depend on the help. The help is a temporary fix and the sooner you can find your inner strength, the sooner the rebuilding process begins. Life is too short to coast, so rise up and conquer it.

Roosevelt once said that we are prisoners of our own minds. Set your goals wisely, maybe consult with a physician, a therapist, a trainer, or even a friend. Then you need a spark to get started. A spark could be a family member or friend encouraging you, or anything that motivates your start. And, if you put your heart, head, soul, and even faith in it, you're giving yourself the best chance of success.

Success is measured in degrees. Say you fall short of your goal, but you gave it everything you had, is that a failure? Not in my eyes. At least you can now move forward without worrying about ever having to look back. Take pride in your efforts and set your sails to a new destination. Embrace the change and make it work for you. The most important thing you can do is surround yourself with positive people, people who are willing to improve everyone around them. Find people who can look past themselves. It is important to have a solid support system.

Make the most of it

"My motto was always to keep swinging. Whether I was in a slump or feeling badly or having trouble off the field, the only thing to do was keep swinging."

—Hank Aaron

I coached my kids right up to college, and I get a lot of questions about that. There is a lot to be learned from playing sports. First, the best players don't always play. Is that fair? No, but it's true. It might be a coach, a child's grades, or maybe it's the child's attitude. The only way to get around this is to prepare your child/children. Trust me the difference is very noticeable. You know who's been paying the price by preparing themselves through practice and videos and who's been slacking. Sure you can wait for someone to be injured to get your moment to play, but wouldn't it be more satisfying to earn that spot yourself. As my father used to say, respect is your greatest reward. The concept that every child who plays should get a trophy is totally wrong in my opinion. Look where that has led us. It lessens the incentive to work hard or be better. This concept applies not only to sporting activities, but to life as well. You want to work hard and strive to be better. Just as in sports, some people are born with natural abilities and excel at their positions, others have to work hard to obtain success. There is that hustle factor that catches the coach's (or the boss's) eye. That person who just won't quit. I believe this is something sports and/or competition can teach you, and you're better for having it.

Some parents take that whole process away from their children by trying to create an easier path for them. I gave my kids the training and tools to succeed, but the path was theirs to navigate. Learning to navigate that path of life is better than any trophy. Both of my sons had a lot of the same abilities, but each had their own approach. Billy used power while Jeremy relied on finesse. Both had the same parents, same training and same coaching, but still utilized a different approach to playing. Both were very successful, so how do you judge which style is better? Sometimes you just need to go with what works for you.

Billy and Jeremy Gannon in the same backfield

My favorite picture of the boys playing football

I have found in life that it's sometimes the little things that matter the most. One of my most successful seasons was a recreational basketball team I coached. We went undefeated and won most games by twenty points or more. We worked hard on fundamentals, but the difference, I believe, came from our weekly parent/child scrimmages. The kids learned heart first-hand from their parents. These die-hard parents would box out, rebound, and even dive on the ground to win. It truly was this group effort that made it such a successful season. The parents would even come early and help with circuits to sharpen the kids' skills. Everyone would get a ton of repetitions. Everyone not only improved their game, but also built a better bond between us all.

A coach's main objective should be putting the best team out there. A good coach assesses each player's skills and potential and puts them in a position to build their confidence. This is exactly what I'm asking you to do in life. Put yourself in the best possible situation by choosing your support system and environment. Find a place where you can thrive.

Take the sport of boxing, for example. Boxers don't just don't turn pro and fight for a title. They work their way through weaker opponents to show and develop their skills. Each step is about sharpening skills and gaining confidence at every level. My Uncle Joe used to say, "Look, learn and leave it," He would tell me to watch what someone was doing, learn from their actions and use that to improve myself if I could, and then leave it at that and focus back on myself.

I had a friend named Jeff who was cut from the baseball team in seventh grade. He was disappointed but knew what he needed to do to make the cut the following year. He was out there the very next day practicing and bettering himself so when the next opportunity arose to try out for the team he'd be ready for it. He wasted no time being bitter or looking back because he knew it would get in the way of what needed to be done and would serve no purpose. After a year of working hard, Jeff achieved his goal and earned a starting position on the team, the same team from which he'd been cut just a year before. Jeff's accomplishment is a great example of what can be achieved if you set a goal and persistently work toward it. There are times when it will feel as if you are swimming against the current trying to accomplish what needs to be done. You might have to strengthen your mind before you strengthen your body. Remember to find that balance. I am still friends with Jeff, and he still makes a huge difference in the lives of people around him. Like Jeff, if you have that focus of the mind, you can move mountains. You can master positive thinking at any point in your life, so never think you are too old to make a meaningful difference in your life or someone else's.

Healing can be a process that is as hard as you want it to be. When we've never gone through a loss, that being physically or maybe the loss of a loved one. I believe we learn from it first. We see what we've lost and how valuable that person was or that body movement was. Those things we took for granted are now in our minds proving their meaning. Second, is accepting it and this seems to be the hardest part in this process. Growing older makes us deal with living with less. Time humbles us all physically, but as I've said before a human life is never replaceable. I've been able to get to the next stage by continuing to enjoy the moments and memories with the people I've lost. I'm thankful for the time I've shared with them. I've seen how much I appreciated the things they taught me, the things they did for me, and most of all the times they shared with me. Third thing is moving past it. Some people find this stage to be the hardest. They find it hard because they can't share those moments with their loved ones anymore. Life doesn't lesson because someone doesn't see something that you've now accomplished. Cus D'Amato trained Mike Tyson to become the heavyweight champion of the world. Taking a raw talent and developing and conditioning him for this role. D'Amato passed away in 1985 and Tyson won the title in 1986. Almost a year later, the title, the goal they both set to accomplish became a reality. Tyson had to focus on the goal and not on the loss to achieve what they both worked for. There are times when we don't see the fruits of our labor come to fruition. You can give up, try another approach, or set your sails for another goal. Because Tyson kept his fire going, he was able to fulfill both of their goals. It's important to not give in until you are ready to move on to the next goal.

Always a pleasure watching these two play

During my adventures in baseball, basketball, and football, I worked extremely hard, but I was never flexible. So when my children were young, I got them involved in martial arts. I made calls to different places and heard many times about the popular program for the three-year black belt. My last call was to sensei Greg Kowalski of New England ninjutsu. As the conversation went on, I knew that he was the right fit. When I asked him about the three-year black belt, he laughed and said, "Your kids won't be black belts in three years, but I will bring them to any dojo in the state and they'll beat any three-year black belt." That's what I wanted in an answer. It's not that you want your kids to pick fights with anyone, but you want them to be able to defend themselves and not have a false sense of themselves because of what color belt they have around their waist. Sensei Kowalski taught my boys how to be gentlemen first, discipline was a requirement in his class.

I strongly recommend martial arts with a good instructor for anyone. Greg Kowalski's stories alone are priceless. He is a master in this art.

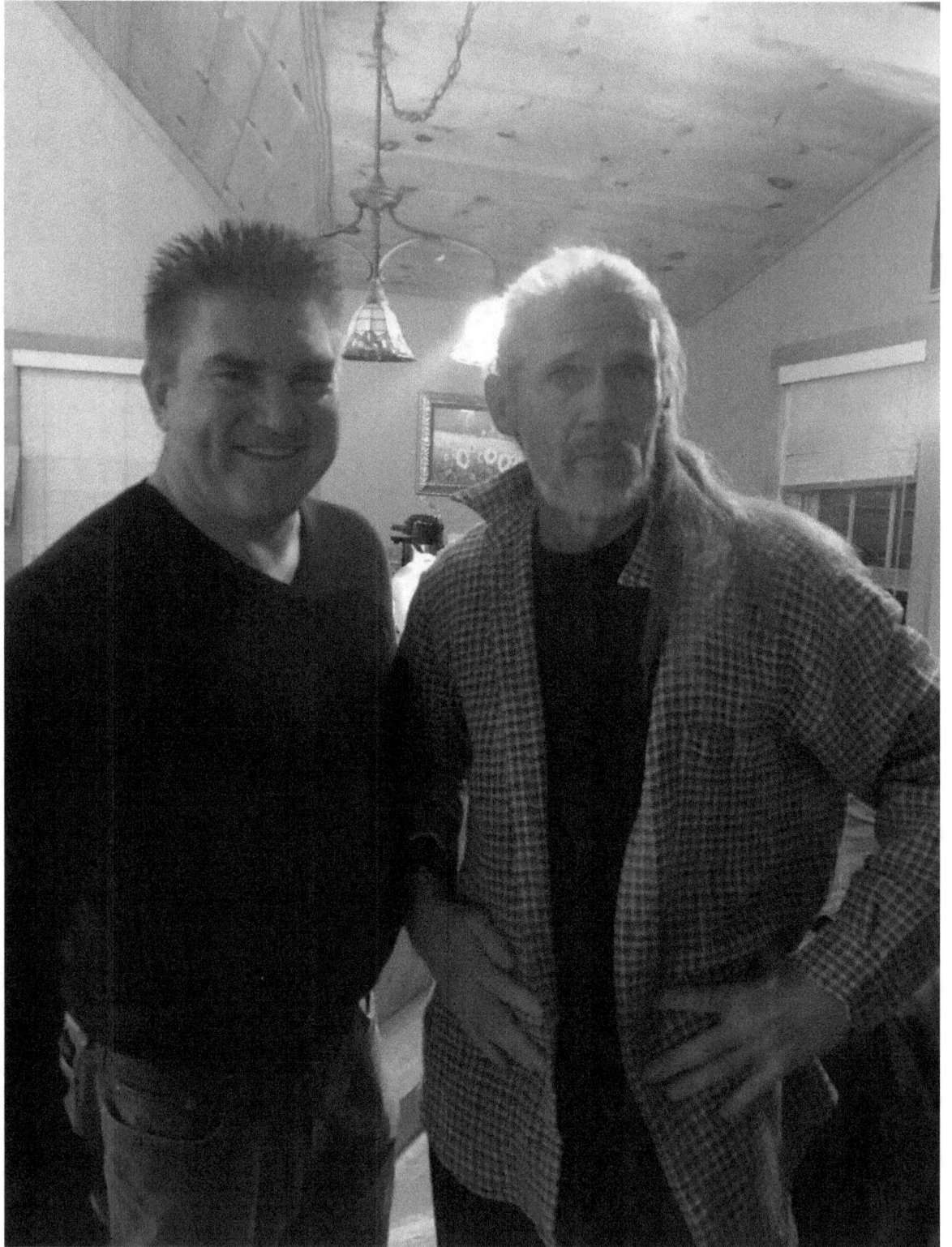

Sensei Greg Kowalski and I

Martial arts can be such a great tool for recovery. It can heighten your skills physically, mentally, and even spiritually, depending on the form you train in. I began training with my sons and quickly noticed the benefits. I was never a physically flexible person, I couldn't even use a riding mower without cramping up. After three months of training with Sensei Kowalski, using a mower was no longer an issue. I learned the value of repetition and a drive for excellence. There's so much you can gain by studying a form for even just a year. Sensei Steve Souchy, who also taught my children martial arts, had some classic quotes. He would say, "Pain is good, it lets you know you're still alive." He didn't offer much sympathy, often telling people to simply "Deal with it."

Whatever the method, the most important lesson is to keep fighting. Sensei Kowalski still checks in with my family and I to see how we're doing when he comes to town. He is a larger than life man who I am lucky enough to call a friend.

These lessons, while they pertain to sports also pertain to life in general. If you teach your children to exercise their minds and beliefs everyday, it becomes second nature to them and will serve them well if they are ever faced with adversity.

When I was growing up my brother-in-law Peter Graeb would say that I would play to the level of my competition just to compete. Maybe it looked like that, and maybe I would give a little, but it was during those games that I was working on my faults, my weaknesses. What I didn't have in talent, I needed to make up for in grit. I had a great support system of people who kept me grounded and persuaded me to keep working hard. I love basketball but I was never the best shooter. Once, when I was thirteen, I attended the Calvin Murphy basketball camp. Calvin is a five-foot, nine-inch National Basketball Association Hall of Famer who at one point held the record for most consecutive free throw shots in the NBA. He took advantage of being able to score points when nobody could guard him. At the time, I was younger, faster, and taller and thought for sure I could prove myself. I hit the first shot, then the second, The third fell into the hoop. I believed at this moment I would just sail to victory, but Calvin didn't think the same way. I never took into consideration his experience and the fact he had been through this before. He stole the ball from me and dribbled deep past the three-point line. I was still up three to nothing in a game to seven. A three-point shot was worth two points in our game.

"Did you ever see a raindrop?" Calvin asked.

"No," I replied.

Calvin explained it was a high-arcing shot. He added a twist, though, he said he wouldn't count it if he hit any part of the rim. The ball went up, and then you heard the snap of the net, no rim. He then made the same offer to me.

It was like Groundhog Day as the second shot looked as if it was a carbon copy of the first one. Next thing I know it was seven to three. Calvin grabbed me before I took two steps away from him and told me this wasn't my game. He told me when it came to basketball, I needed a team environment to utilize my skills.

He told me his shooting abilities were God given and that I needed to use my God-given gifts. I took Calvin advice and did what I needed to do just to make the team and that required more work on my behalf.

There aren't many things in life that just fall into our laps without some effort from us. Life takes someone who " doesn't have the word *quit* in their vocabulary," according to my Uncle Joe. "That special someone willing to face all their fears to make it happen." He liked to tell me that while no one is afraid to win, you also can't be afraid to lose. Both he and my father repeatedly told me to focus on the task at hand. This was a lesson I learned well.

My first day of varsity football practice proved the value of this lesson. I kept screwing up the footwork for the handoffs to the running backs. The more frustrated I got, the more I lost my focus. I was upset with my performance and when I called my uncle that night, he told me not to let the mistakes seem more than they were.He told me to practice the footwork over and over. He predicted that I would become more relaxed with every repetition. He told me if I wanted this dream bad enough that I couldn't let anything or anyone get in my way. As our conversation ended, he told me to practice the footwork for another hour at a slow pace and to concentrate on every detail. I did as he instructed and with every repetition I gained confidence and speed.

This is a good example of how one can learn from failure, whether in sports or in life in general. I realized I needed to focus a little more to develop my skills. I needed to set aside the fear and doubt in order to succeed.

 My father lived by the American proverb, "Don't judge a man until you've walked a mile in his shoes," and he passed it on to me. He never wanted me to get caught up in drama, but to rise above it, or look past it as best I could. If there was one saying I heard more than any other, it was, "Prove them wrong."

When I was in little league, I was put in the outfield on the all-star team after I had played catcher all year long for my regular team. Three practices in, I was frustrated because I thought I was being punished because my father didn't coach. I vented to my dad and he told me not to worry where the coach was putting me and be happy I was on the team in the first place. He pointed out that there were a lot of kids who would love to have my problem, but they were sitting home because they didn't make the team. This was one of my first lessons on changing my perspective and being thankful for what I did have, not what I didn't.

My father laid out three steps for me. First make the team; second, make a difference; and third, and most important, make them respect you. My father always pushed me to think about more than myself. He would never allow me to doubt my talents but would point out reasons why things were the way they were. Maybe the coach needed me in the outfield more than he needed me anywhere else. Once again, a sports lesson that also applies to life.

.

Look Back but always move Forward

"Without continual growth and progress, such words as improvement, achievement, and success have no meaning."

—Benjamin Franklin

I wrote this book because people wanted to know how I navigated and survived the difficult times in my life. When the accident happened, as you can imagine, a lot of lives changed immediately. I can only speak for Matt Escoto and myself when I say it changed us physically, mentally, and even spiritually. This event not only shattered *us,* but also the worlds of a good amount of people around us.

Why is it so much easier to talk ourselves into darkness? We need to believe it's just as easy to talk ourselves out of darkness. Why stay stagnant? Today could be the day where you start the ripple effect and begin to make a difference. Become that example for someone, or at least just for you. Don't keep yourself in your comfort zone. It is through discomfort that we grow. When we try to control the chaos around us, we will eventually see we can't. It's like going into a gym and doing the same routine everyday. Yes, you will be in shape for your routine but you aren't preparing yourself for anything else or anything new. Every once in awhile you need to change things up. Your body will feel the pain because it's challenged in a different way.

Before my son started boxing, he could easily play four quarters of a football game with no problems. His body was conditioned for that game for which he had so vigorously trained, but when he began training for a boxing match he realized that this particular challenge called for different training. While his football training was not wrong, it would not help him in this situation. Certain things in life call for different approaches and that's important for us to see. It's all about perspective.

It's important to surround yourself with people who want you to pick up the pieces. The accident was the first time in my life that I lost someone close to me. He was my best friend and he had so many doors in life that were wide open to him. I was seventeen and had just learned how fragile life was. After the accident, I was swimming in a sea of doubt; confusion and questions filled my mind. Both Matt and I had to learn to heal our minds as well as our bodies.

Do I revisit those painful times once in a while? Yes. I chose to see them more as reminders of how much ground I've gained, rather than reminders of what I've lost. See the difference in perspective? When you're heading for the finish line you don't look back at the starting blocks because you know exactly where you started. Instead, you look forward to where you are headed. You don't mourn the ground you've lost, as that's behind you now, but you continue to move forward, gaining ground with each step.

For a time after the accident, things weren't going my way. Prognoses were being tossed around from doctor to doctor, but all I could see was that my life had changed and I had no control over it. I was in a pretty gloomy place. My father had told me to stay home that January night, yet I chose to go out. Things would have been different had I stayed home. and I felt I had let a lot of people down. Somehow, though, I found a way to hold on to a glimmer of hope. I didn't always have a firm grasp on it, but it was a start. I stopped buying into what I was told I wouldn't be able to do and started buying into what I could do. Disappointment became my driving fuel. I needed to pick myself up. *Can't* and *couldn't* were replaced with *could*. As I say in the beginning of the book, where there's a will there is a way. I used a calendar to track my gains. Each week I strived to win four days. Four days meant I had won the week. Three weeks meant I had won the month. (It was important to me to see the progress along the way.

The first few weeks were the toughest because they were filled with sorrow, and I believe this is true of all tragedies. It's okay to take the time to grieve, give that gift to yourself, but at some point, you need to transition into healing. Surround yourself with people who will pull you out of the depths of that empty well. Find that ray of hope to build on, reach for it and hold on until you achieve your goals.

I started writing movie scripts while in the hospital to keep my mind occupied and away from the negative. There was a lot of downtime where my mind would try and focus on the negative, I couldn't let that happen. The longer you can keep those negative thoughts out, the quicker you will correct the situation. Time heals, but it can also haunt you if you allow it to. There are so many triggers that can send you off in a negative direction. Holding on to the smallest bits of hope is better than giving in to the negative demons that will arise on a daily basis. You need to develop tough skin, put the blinders on, and have that laser precision focus to succeed.

While losing my daughter was the hardest thing I have ever experienced, the car accident posed my biggest challenge physically. I was in great shape at the time because of my love of football and because of my age.

When I arrived at the first hospital that evening of January 20, the doctor told me he wanted to amputate my left leg. An hour and a half later I was at Yale New Haven Hospital being put through a battery of tests then a ten-hour surgery. When I woke up, my left leg was still there. Things were already better than they said it would be just fifteen hours earlier. I was beat up, but I was far from done, and from giving up. First and foremost, I was blessed with still being alive. Two, I still had my leg. Can you see why I had plenty to build on? Was there a long hard road ahead of me? Yes, but I was given the opportunity to continue, regardless of where the road would lead me. I was also very fortunate that I didn't use pain medication during my recovery and therefore did not run the risk of becoming dependent upon pills. So many people struggle with this through no fault of their own and I am very aware of how lucky I am. This pattern of positive keeps appearing in my life as long as I keep looking for it. You have to keep reminding yourself about the positives in your life, even if they are very minimal. Take it one second, one hour, one day at a time. Life is all about overcoming loss—physically, mentally, and spiritually. It's your goal to keep contributing daily to these goals until you are whole again.

Prepare yourself for Pain

"Don't lie to yourself, prepare yourself for pain."

—William Gannon, Sr.

My father would always say, He taught me that going into a situation knowing what you are up against or knowing what needs to be done can keep the stress at a tolerable level. You try to prepare for every scenario. I am not saying it's easy, but if you can focus on your gains and not your pains you will speed up your recovery process.

I understand it is not as easy as it sounds, but let's look at that. Why does it have to be so difficult? If we can talk ourselves right into a deep, dark place, why can't we reverse that thinking and talk ourselves right back out? Again, it's all about perspective.

I remember my brother-in-law, Peter Graeb, saying after the accident "There's always somebody worse." This simple statement can serve to remind you that wherever you are in your life, you are not starting at rock bottom. It is also reassuring to know that you aren't the only one who has ever faced a situation capable of pulling the life out of you. I received many uplifting letters after the accident. I kept these letters in my nightstand and would read them multiple times. They let me know people were seeing me as an example and not a victim.

When things got rough for me and I would start to lose my way, I thought about those people who were there for me. When I couldn't do it for myself, I did it for them.

I followed my father's advice and prepared myself for the pain of failure. Now that I'm a parent I see what a tough position I put my parents and a lot of people through. I knew as I was working on my dream of being a professional football player that I was more likely to fail than succeed. I accepted that I wouldn't ever be the same player I was before the accident and that I was more susceptible to injury now, but that didn't stop me. I was all in to achieve my goal for two reasons. The first was the challenge. No one thought it could be done. The second was closure. I had given so much to my dream of playing professional football that I needed to know it was over before I could move onto the next journey in my life. I did play again, but it wasn't the same. I left that field with no doubt that my sails were going into a different direction at this point.

The next obstacle I faced was my darkest. We lost my daughter Danielle. What made it even worse was that she didn't leave us because of any physical ailments or diseases; she was a healthy baby who lost her chance at life due to the arrogance of a doctor. The loss of our daughter was compounded by the loss of my wife Agnes's uterus at the same time. Losing the ability to have more children brought Agnes to rock bottom. No matter where I turned or what I did, I came up empty for answers on how I could help her. Things were uncertain to say the least. I was close to hopeless and felt so helpless.

My faith helped. I have a framed print of the poem, "Footprints" in my room. It reminds me every day that God will carry me when I can no longer carry myself. At the time, I was just trying to find the right words to try and make sense of all that had happened. I held back my tears as much as I could to try to be the pillar of strength for my family.

I felt as if my back was on the ropes and my only options were to be knocked out, knocked down, or fight back. I felt that if I failed, it would cost me my family. That was where my mind was and I am grateful I still had my faith in me to wage a fight. I prayed a lot and I knew a lot of people were praying for me. As I said before, it was my son Billy who snapped me out of my sorrow and showed me that beacon of light. It took a child to show me not to overthink a situation. At that moment I knew the best way to go to war against a monumental loss was to attack it with a profound love.

I was determined to save my family. This was not a fight I was willing to lose. The hardest and most important thing I needed to do was build my wife's mindset back up to where she needed to be. A family isn't about one person, it's about all of you. I needed to show Agnes how important and loved she was as a mother, wife, daughter, sister, and so on. I needed her to focus on the family we had and not on what we had lost. Was it easy? No! Two hours every night for a year and a half I would build her up, heal her wounds, and show her how much she was needed and loved.

When you see yourself as insufficient you can't see yourself overcoming even the smallest of odds. I would tell her she was too strong to just collapse. I told her over and over that there were four other people who needed her. Every day I would show her how much ground she had gained.

Yes, there were the moments of setbacks, but I would constantly tell her healing was greater than her hurt. We would watch home videos or bring out pictures of her smiling. I was basically repeating the same thing night after night,, but that is what it took. Finally, she started to believe me. Everything I was saying started to make sense to her. When she saw it, she never looked back.

You can either fight the healing or you can fight the hurting. That should be a very easy choice for anyone to make. Decide what's important around you and when you get into that right frame of mind you'll win your war.

When we lost Danielle we visited her plot every night after dinner, rain or shine, it didn't matter. I would watch my wife's demeanor change as we arrived at the plot and I knew this wasn't helping in her recovery. It was keeping her stuck in a moment. Sometimes we don't see what's holding us back. We think we are holding on to something, but in fact we are denying ourselves the freedom we need to find our purpose or free our lives from the shackles of a situation. Of course everyone is different, but sometimes we need to limit our return to the past. It was my job to show my wife how much more her future was. I needed her to see past the hurt in her heart and mind. I needed a plan.

Our response to our problems is often a huge part of our battle. I believe the quicker we can face our situations and fears, the quicker we conquer them. Where do you see yourself when the going gets tough? I want you to think about how you would cope with a bad situation. I do my best to figure out a game plan for how I can stay in the fight. It's a hard thing to keep moving forward when you're not in control of the issue. How do you cope with things at these points in life? You can return to those things that brought yourself levity before you came face to face with this problem. Have faith, you'll get to the finish line, you'll find that way to win, to see life with worth again.

I don't have the option to fail anymore. People expect me to succeed. I've gotten through those hard times because God has given me the strength to redeem myself. Keep dreaming, find the new hungers in life, and never give up on hope.

When a person can see their worth it gives them more of a reason to fight. At the end of that same year, Agnes began to bounce back with a new love of life. She relished every moment she had with her family. As low as she was, she was able to muster up some strength when I lost my father. She knew I didn't have much left in my tank and, in a way, I think helped her see her own strength. Again, I believe when we can focus on someone or something else we can find that meaning that shows us that purpose again. Always look for that thing to pull you from the darkness.

My father was the glue of our family. He was able to keep us from going for each other's throats. He loved providing for us and did so no matter what the price or the toll it took on him. When we lost him, I spent a lot of time thinking about the lessons he taught me. I also thought about all the new situations life would send my way that I wouldn't be able to bounce off him anymore.

My father and I spoke everyday when he was alive. I didn't feel ready to go on without him. Losing a daughter *and* a father in one year tested my metal, but it also made me practice what I was preaching. I knew what I had lost, but I also knew what was left in me. I picked up the pieces and continued to do the things that would make them proud. My father left tough shoes to fill, whether in sports, work, or, most of all, life. My father was all about family, and the last thing he would want is seeing me not going the distance for mine. I wasn't about to disappoint him now.

Two years later, also in December, my Uncle Joe Kuczo passed away. He and my father had given me so much and were instrumental in me being the man I was. I recall sitting in front of the Christmas tree that year reflecting on what they had instilled in me and realizing that that was the real gift. I remembered the great times we had together and I knew at that moment that I needed to give my all to my family.

I had no idea at the time what that would entail. I had hoped that maybe things would settle down for us. That maybe we'd had our share of tragedy. I was wrong. In mid-summer 2005, Agnes and I were watching our son Billy's baseball game when she suddenly collapsed. Two nurses quickly came to her aid and we all noticed her face drooping on the left side. I came close to losing it, this couldn't be happening. I remember talking myself out of fainting. I knew I had to gather the strength to be there for Agnes. As people are wont to do in such situations, I went on autopilot. I didn't feel anything going on around me. It was as if I had blinders on and earplugs in. I don't know how I got to the hospital, but you do what you have to in those times. I told myself that Agnes was such a strong woman, so there was hope. It was not meant to be, though. On July 3, 2005, Agnes passed away from an aneurysm at the age of thirty-three.

We left the hospital as a family shattered that fateful day. Our Norman Rockwell life no longer familiar. I remember my mother grabbing my arm and telling me not to give up my faith. While I did question God's plan for me at times, I never gave up on Him. The Bible is full of stories about people who were suffering and struggling through life. My faith gave me strength. Faith is about believing and trusting in God. I went to bed that night thinking the loss was just too much. I couldn't replace what Agnes gave and meant to the children. Those magical Christmas or Easter mornings would now be missing this amazing angel in their lives. My mind was taking me to all the things we had lost as a family. I was struggling through what seemed an endless time when I thought of her, Agnes, in heaven with Danielle. When it was just the two of us in the hospital room together after she had collapsed, I knew if Agnes saw Heaven and our little angel, she wasn't coming back. This is another example of where my faith allows me to find something positive on a very modest scale. This was our reality now. I had three children who were relying on me to continue to be not only their father, but now even more. So together we healed. The kids went to counseling to make sure they were processing everything in a healthful way. We relied on our faith, as well, to help us heal. Agnes had filled their hearts, for the short time she was here, with enough love to last a lifetime.

I can say it a thousand times and it never seems like enough, so I'll say it again. Children are resilient. My kids made it through with very few hiccups. Of course there were days that challenged us, but you deal with those days as they come. You brace yourself for certain dates that will inevitably make you stumble, but you face them as they come.

I remember one particular Mother's Day. The Friday before, my daughter Casey was taking a reading test. She consistently maintained an A average in school, but she barely passed this test. Perhaps it was timing or maybe it wasn't. I was called in to see the school counselor and Casey's teacher. I was told about all the issues my daughter was having in school. I was confused. I had believed she only had two issues—her mother and her sister not being with us anymore. I told the counselor to not make things worse than they already were. I was told my daughter didn't cry enough. First off, while there is nothing wrong with crying, there comes a time when tears of pain have to take a backseat to the joys of life. It's not good to allow tears to continue to control your life. Like any negative thing, you have to get past it and move toward a positive outcome. Don't give in to what I call reasons of retreat. Those times where we throw in the towel and collapse under the pressure of pain. You can surrender to your pain and sorrow and spend a lifetime reliving that moment until you look back on your own life and see and say was it worth it? I spoke with a woman who just lost her son. It devastated her, and rightly so. When she saw that time began suppressing the grief and she was able to focus a little clearer, she started talking about starting a scholarship foundation in her son's name. I told her that was a great idea and she should start one to keep his memory going and give her a new purpose.

I can't even say this was something I came up with. I got this idea from my neighbors Matt and Jan Coyle who lost their daughter Patricia Coyle on Pan Am Flight 103 over Lockerbie, Scotland. A terrorist concealed a bomb in a radio cassette player in a suitcase that caused the explosion, an act, which claimed the lives of two hundred and seventy people on December 21, 1988. This moment hit our town hard at the time; suddenly you can't say "it doesn't happen to us." There's a bench in Patricia's honor outside the front entrance of Sheehan High School. A memorial garden was also constructed outside of the Wallingford Public Library. I spoke with Mr. Coyle asking his permission to include this story in my book. We both couldn't believe that thirty years goes by so fast. The Coyle's are amazing people who started a memorial scholarship fund in their daughter's name. They are bringing something positive out of a tragedy. I've seen first hand how this foundation has made an impact on the recipients of this scholarship. My son Jeremy was awarded the Patricia M. Coyle Memorial Scholarship in 2015. It was a real honor for him to receive the scholarship from Mr. and Mrs. Coyle. The Coyle's have reinforced my belief that good things can stem from a bad moment. You'll read about people put in your path many times in this book. I was lucky to be neighbors with such strong people with hearts of gold. It's crazy to think two of the most tragic moments to happen to students at Sheehan High School would end up neighbor's just years later. Find the kind of people like the Coyle's to show you a way to overcome in a heartfelt and meaningful way.

I've seen this become a successful tool a few times now. I coached a boy in Little League when he was around ten or eleven years old. I later found out he passed away right after high school. Like any parent, his father was devastated by the loss and wanted to start a scholarship in his son's name. I believe this to be a great way to keep a person's name, or in some cases their cause, relevant. I think this is a win-win for everyone who is involved. This is no different than an organ donor program. It allows someone to benefit from someone else's loss. Abraham Lincoln once said, In the end, it's not the years in your life that count. It's the life in your years." President Lincoln didn't always have the easiest path, but he made the most of certain situations. Remember it's not how bad you want something, but rather how hard you are willing to work for it. You'll hear athletes say it's tough getting there, but even tougher to remain on top.

Replace the Bitter

It is a simple but sometimes forgotten truth that the greatest enemy to present joy and high hopes is the cultivation of retrospective bitterness.
—Robert Menzies

I am often asked why I am not bitter about the things that happened in my life. My answer is always the same: I am not bitter because I am thankful for the opportunities and experiences I was given. On January 20, 1989, I was pulled out of a car and blessed with the opportunity to see another day. I just never thought I had the right to complain. I was given this gift of seeing the world from a different perspective. I face the problems in front of me as they come.

It's always important to remember that you are not the only one suffering. Pain is all around us, some people are just better at hiding it than others. Some are subtle about asking for help. I recall scrolling through Facebook one Christmas Eve. I noticed a buddy had posted that he was starting to get the Christmas blues. I gave him a call and asked how he was doing. This is the same person who got me into the Christmas spirit in 2019 by saying he was happy people had put up their Christmas lights the week prior to Thanksgiving. This guy would do anything for you. When we got past the initial greetings he went on to tell me how Christmas just wasn't the same for him since he had lost his wife about twenty years ago. He worried about his daughter and how it was affecting her. When we lose someone we love, special days are different, and will never be the same. That being said, different doesn't have to be bad. This is the time to make new traditions. Maybe it's a change of venue, or maybe someone else has to take the reins now, but whatever it is you can make it something of which your loved one would have been proud. Traditions are meant to be passed down, sometimes it's just a little sooner than we'd like. The most important thing is to find a way to be happy again. Give new memories a chance. Sometimes we need to embrace the change. When I hung up the phone from my call with my friend, I didn't think I had changed his mind, but I was pretty sure I got him thinking. The next day he posted on Facebook about how he and his daughter had never talked about their loss and how they were feeling because they were trying to give each other space. Each of them thought it was too painful for the other. I learned later that when they did talk, his daughter told him that she felt that when her mom died, part of him died too. She felt that only a small part of him was "there" at Christmas time. This woke him up, he said, and he realized it was time to start making new traditions.

Making new traditions and living your new way doesn't mean the pain just disappears, but it does mean you're finding a way to live with it. You are moving forward toward this new beginning. I believe with time, love, and laughter, you will find healing.

Storms come at times and they can devastate, but they don't last forever. There will be times when you have to pick up the pieces and start over. You have to believe you can make it out of the situation. You need to see that every step moves you forward. I am forty-eight years old and have had one bad January 20, one bad April 11 and so forth. I don't shut down on those days but I slow down. I make a point to make new pleasant memories on those days. I used to buy flowers and visit the graves on those anniversary dates, but then I thought these loves meant more than tragedy. When my mother was diagnosed with cancer, my approach changed. This was the first time where a loved one's passing wasn't sudden in my life.. The down side to a situation like this is having to watch your loved one struggle, knowing they are in pain. The good side (for a lack of a better description) is having the chance to spend time with them to reflect on your lives. Isn't it funny how much time you can find when you find out a friend or loved one has limited time remaining? All those times when you were too busy or had something better to do all begin to pale in comparison to spending time with them now. My mother showed a great deal of strength and used her remaining time to meet with all of her children and grandchildren to tell us what we meant to her and what she could see us doing in our futures. Moments like that are true gifts.

I have a story about a mother and a daughter. The daughter was working on a homework assignment, having waited until the day before it was due. Stress levels were high, and when she went to print the assignment, there was a problem with the WiFi and the printer wasn't receiving the signal from the laptop. Both mom and daughter tried to get it to work, but the printer wasn't gathering the information it needed. A small problem began to grow way beyond what it should have. Hurtful words were being thrown back and forth. Things were getting ugly. These things tend to happen when we focus on the problem and not the solution. I looked at the situation from a different perspective, I thought about possible solutions. Now, I don't know a lot about computers and printers, but I had once watched my son use an HDMI cord to fix our slow wifi and weak signal. I asked the mom and daughter if they had a cord and suggested they give that a try. It worked and the homework was printed. You would never think that something so little could cause so much fallout, but it happens all the time. It's easy to hurt the people around us, especially when we focus on the problem and not the solution.

Why do we so often sink to throwing insults at each other when we should be supporting one another. Why does it take the loss of someone for us to see their worth? Think about that and don't jump to insult next time, stop, take a deep breath and focus on the issue and not the insults.

So what do you do when you are wrestling with your emotions? I recommend looking for balance. Too much anger isn't good, so find a reason to bring yourself back to the surface. When tragedy hits, we tend to disconnect. I remember when we lost our daughter, Danielle, we were in such disbelief. We couldn't make sense of things. We were hurting in every way possible. Our son Jeremy's birthday was approaching soon. My mother offered to have Jeremy's birthday party at her house to keep the stress off of Agnes. When Agnes arrived at my parent's house, she didn't have much in her. She looked as if she just existed. My parents, with the help of Jeremy's aunts and uncles made his birthday very special. My mother said it best: He was king for the day, his smile melted all our hearts. Even Agnes managed a smile. There's nothing like a child's resilience to show us how to keep moving forward. He was so happy and we all needed that moment of levity. It was a hint of what could be behind the dark gloomy clouds that were lingering.

When in the depths of despair, we sometimes find it easier to pull someone into the pit than to pull ourselves out of it. Reliving thoughts of your past can hinder your recovery, but only if you let them. As I've said countless times before, you can grieve what you have lost, but you *must* celebrate what you have left. Life is what you make of it. You have a blank pardon in front of you, it's up to you to sign it and release yourself from your personal prison sentence. Surviving isn't easy, but it is rewarding. Find that reason to flourish again. This book is written to help you to recover and make a difference from today until the day you die. I think it's best to let the happiness back into your heart and the pain and hurt leave it.

Casey and Jeremy enjoying the summer day. Never forget the good times.

What Are You Seeing?

"I have never started a poem yet whose end I knew."

—Robert Frost

Everyday we get up and look in the mirror at an image of ourselves. Now ask yourself, what do you see? Do you see the person you want to be, or the person someone else wants you to be? Think about that for a minute. If you're not seeing the person you want to be, you may have some work to do. Think of who you want to be, where you want to be and then make a plan to get there. Give this plan everything you have. If you can do this, you will start to become more comfortable with and confident in yourself. Find your support system and lean on them, use them to help yourself. When I was recovering, my doctor, Dr. Frank Palermo, told me that thirty pounds of pressure on a cane can support three hundred pounds of body weight. The right tools or support can make what you see as impossible, very possible.

We've all seen professional athletes who are in the limelight for a couple of years and then their careers suddenly come to a halt. I believe the main reason for this is that they didn't continue to do the work. It is easy to get complacent in where we are and what we have accomplished, but the work shouldn't end. Your body changes, your life changes. Just like any athlete, we have to go out every day in hopes of gaining new ground. Sure, there will be problems and you will face resistance of many kinds, but you keep digging in, you keep working.

When one way stops working, you find another way to make an impact. I called my first book *To Lose But Not Fail* as a way of showing that it did not matter what tragedies or obstacles came my way, I found a way through. I lost a lot, but I didn't let myself fail for long. We all need to find a way to overcome, and be an example to not only ourselves, but others as well.

My children made it easy for me to pick myself up and continue on the best I could. I had to accept my physical injuries, but I refused to let them affect the other aspects of my life. Do I ever think of where I could be? Of course. But where I am outweighs these thoughts all of the time. I see myself as blessed for being where I am. Was a dream taken from me? Yes it was, but I grew in so many other ways.

When it comes to healing, we are all on our own clock. If ten people lost a loved one on the same day, there would be ten different ways and length of time needed to heal. There is no single method or length of healing for people. There is no scale that says a parent takes a year, a grandparent takes six months, and an aunt or uncle three months. Everyone heals in their own time, in their. I knew this woman who lost her father. She did a great job making his last months special. Everything a father could ask for from his daughter, she did. Was it tough on her? Of course, but she got it done. The treatments and doctor visits may seem to be a burden at the time, but as time goes on you'll see how rewarding they were. Time spent with someone in his or her last years or months or even days is and should be looked on as very special moments that will be cherished by you for years to come. When time is limited, we begin to speak from the heart and we notice the true meaning of life.

When my friend's father died, she wanted to write his eulogy, a task that is never easy. Limiting all those meaningful moments to a few pages really felt impossible at the time. Where to start? How to finish? My friend authored a great tribute to her father. There wasn't a dry eye in the room, even after only a paragraph in. The thing I was most proud of was that she overcame her doubt and got up there and got through it. The room was full of family and friends wiping tears from their eyes as the tissue boxes emptied. Her tribute had resonated with everyone in that room. She returned to her seat with relief and a pride of what she just accomplished. She did all this with a lot on her plate. She hosted the gathering after the service. She handed out obituaries to the family members who were from out of town, made sure everyone had eaten. She allowed everyone else to just grieve and start their healing processes. Being so close to her father, my friend then took her own time to recover. I watched and learned something from her during this process. She would often say, "I'm not you." I had never thought of it that way. She was right, we all heal at our own speed.

It's about finding a way to smile again. That doesn't mean that the missing doesn't matter, it just means the life left to live needs to be addressed too.

I believe in balance, some may call it karma. I think you reap what you sow. The challenge is in building yourself up rather than tearing others around you down. We all influence the people around us. I know some people will not agree with me, or they are too self absorbed to care, but we all need to look up to someone, especially when we fall; and we all need to be that person for others when and if we can.

Humility keeps us grounded; it keeps us moving in the right direction. There is nothing wrong with improving yourself or making a product better. However, pass on what you have learned to bring someone else's dreams to fruition, or even just to improve their lives for just that one moment.

My father passed away in December 2001 and I still think of him all the time. I still hear him pointing me in the right direction, keeping me on my toes. I keep working on the house he built, the house in which I now live. I'm not in this house to relive memories of the past, although that does happen, I'm mostly here to build new memories and stories with who's here and who's on their way. The house I'm in has been the home of three generations of my family. It's strange how that's lost something today. The world has lost where it came from. We've chosen individualism as our new normal, and look at the direction that has taken us.

When my sister Maryanne and my brother-in-law Pete moved out of their old house, my sister asked me if I could try and dig out a Christmas tree my father had planted years ago. The tree was just a sapling when he planted it but had grown to a good six feet. I said I would do the best I could with the size of the tree, but couldn't promise anything. I gave it my all to get a good-size ball for the root system, but by the time I dragged it to the car, most of the roots had been exposed to the air and didn't stand much of a chance of making it. I arrived at their new house where they already had a hole dug with water in it. We placed the tree in the hole and covered the roots and hoped for the best. Truthfully? I didn't think the tree was going to make it, but it did, even after all it had been through. It was meant to be. These days, that tree stands at least sixteen feet tall. They decorate it with lights every year and every now and again a cardinal likes to take a break on a branch.

We were all able to keep that memory going. Some would argue that it's better to let go. I say, "Why not let the good memories last"? My sisters and I see cardinals as a reminder of my parents. We believe it's a forget-me-not sent from above until we all meet again. I am who I am because of my parents, and I love to remember where I came from and what they gave me. We revisit those special moments a lot more when we lose someone we love. Moving on is not about forgetting, but rather accepting and keeping the love, laughter, and lessons in your heart and head. Does time heal? Time can do whatever you want it to. Time can heal if you work with it, or it can torture you if you allow it to.

People remember all the great times and all the hard moments, it's the stuff in-between we tend to forget. A friend of mine, Robert Naccarato, once said to me as he stood in my parent's house, "I bet this house has a lot of great memories." It absolutely does and I hope the best is yet to come. My goal now is to make more of the in-betweens. I know how fragile life is and I want to make the most of every moment I have left.

In August 2019, two of my sisters and I went to a party with our parents' best friends, Henry and Nancy Ohr. Another friend, Butch Laughlin, was also there. We spent hours sharing stories from the past. There were no tears, just smiles and laughter. That's the point I try to make to those in recovery. Find the laughter out of the loss. Find a way to smile again. Take a vacation, watch a comedy, start a project, whatever works. That pathway to a peaceful mind can rest in you if you allow it.

It's sometimes tough to be around me because I make the most of the moments I have left. I don't dive into relationships. I take my time, but then I am all in. I don't like throwing relationships away. I'm old school and want to work things out. I had a girlfriend once who didn't want me to have Agnes's pictures in my house. She would constantly say I was stuck in the past because I wouldn't take them down. I wasn't stuck in the past, I appreciated what I had from those days. The life Agnes and I built and the foundation we both gave our children will last a lifetime.

That's why the visit with my parents' best friends was so important. When my parents passed away, these people kept us in their lives, and that speaks to the love and respect they had for our parents. Bonds like that transcend a loss. Time may take us from each other eventually, but even time can't break the bond of love, it continues to exist if only in your heart and head.

My good friend Tara Comiskey always tells me to take a vacation. Tara has been to all fifty states and to numerous places abroad as well. She has a point, we never know when our time will be up, so you can't keep putting off your goals. I've heard and seen pictures of the Grand Canyon from multiple people and they all say the same thing, that words and pictures can't compare to the feeling of being there and seeing it first-hand. We always have people in our lives who point out those little things we might want to start paying attention to. Someday soon my friend Tara might just get a postcard from somewhere other than Wallingford, Connecticut.

Always a good time with Mr. & Mrs. Ohr

Butch Loughlin and I having some laughs

Right around the end of June, 2019, I woke up one morning with swollen hands. My first thought was I had lyme disease. I headed to a clinic, where the attending physician took my blood pressure, said I was a walking time bomb and that I needed to get to the emergency room immediately. I'm not a big fan of going to the hospital, but I'll go if things go south. They took me right in and started the battery of tests. My heart was good. My lungs were good. My kidneys were also good. My blood pressure was not. Even though I was in pretty good shape other than my ailments from the car accident, my blood pressure was in the danger zone. I'm still recovering from my blood pressure while I'm writing this chapter. I could always lift pretty heavy weights. Although since I turned forty, I did change my routines and did limit my weights. It was hard for me to accept I could only lift twenty-five pounds. Guess I'm thrown another challenge. I will say my sister did tell me to get checked. I'm old school again and if it's not broke, then don't fix it. Not the best move on my behalf. It's definitely a tougher fix then I expected with age being a greater factor, but i'm getting there. I never experimented with drugs, I don't smoke, and I drink only a handful of times per year, so I thought I took pretty good care of myself, but even if we do everything right, we can still inherit health issues.

So I live and learn. This is a minor setback due to my lack of action. I will move forward with the same approach I always have. Again, it's about making adjustments and finding that formula to get moving in the right direction. Being diagnosed with high blood pressure has shown me how much more I had just a few weeks ago. I certainly took my mobility for granted. Some days I get up and feel great and other mornings it's a struggle. Some days I need extra time just to get out of the car. There were also days I would have to reach for the phone with my other arm because one was so weak. I continue to fight the only way I know how. I try to win the days, then the week, then the month and then the year. I won't win every day, but winning four out of the seven days gets me a week. My point in telling you all of this is to show you that you can do it too. Sometimes you have to push the pain aside to get better. Always give yourself the best chance to heal. I have no doubt I'll beat this new challenge, and I have no doubt you will beat yours too.

Bitter is a bad gear in which to get stuck. When you view your life in terms of what others have that you haven't, you are doing yourself a disservice. Instead, try to view your life in what you have, not what you don't. Be proud of who and what you are or can be. We all slip once in a while, but it's those who can move past the bitterness and find the focus in themselves who achieve great things.

The night of the accident took so much from so many people I love. But it gave us a few gifts as well. We lost a good friend that night when Marc Izzo died. To this day, I believe Marc took the brunt of the impact in order to give Matt and I a better chance of survival. While I went to Yale that night for my surgeries and treatments, Matt was airlifted to Hartford Hospital for his. Twice that night, Matt's heart stopped. He was in a coma for days after. When he finally woke up, his memory of that night and six months prior to the accident was a blur. But when his father asked him how he was feeling he told him that I was still alive, but Marc was no longer with us. Wanting to know how he knew this, his father questioned him again. He told him that he had been in heaven and he saw me walking into clouds. He then said he looked in the other direction and saw Jesus Christ walking Marc into the pearly gates. Marc turned and told Matt to follow me because it wasn't his time. This experience changed his life, and mine. His faith became very important in his life. He even thanked Jesus Christ in his yearbook. I always had a strong faith, but this story reinforced it tenfold.

While some people question these types of stories, you'll never tell me otherwise. I was in the death seat in the car that night. I was in and out of that car seven times that day. I never put my seat belt on. The eighth time, two minutes before the accident I put it on because I noticed Marc putting his on. That simple choice saved my life. I've seen or heard too many of these types of experiences to just ignore them or consider them coincidence.

Matt and I talked about these things often and we both agreed things certainly happen for reasons. He came over to my house one summer afternoon to swim with me. After the swim we got so involved in talking that the next thing I knew I was running late for a date with a girl named Melanie Winn. Melanie was a head turner to say the least. She was also smart and had a great heart. I asked Matt if he wanted to join us. He agreed and we all went to the movies, we all had a good time, and then I dropped both of them at their houses. That following Monday, Matt asked me about Melanie and I knew. He was in love. Melanie and I had only been on two dates, including the one with Matt. I knew it was over for me. There was something between them that was so special that I had no right to interfere. Besides, it seems God had other plans for me. A few weeks later, on Marc's birthday, I went on a blind date and met Agnes, my future wife and mother of my kids.

I was going to dinner one night and as we were waiting to order, I was talking to a friend whose brother was widowed and who had just lost a second son. He lost two sons and a wife in fifteen years. She was worried about her brother because he wouldn't see a counselor to ease the pain. She asked if I would call him and see if I might be able to help him. I took his number and went to my car. We talked for over an hour. We went through everything, exchanging stories and emotions and how it was possible to move past losses and continue on with life. The next day his sister called me and thanked me for listening. She asked her brother what the difference is talking to a counselor or to me. He said, "Because he's been through it." Sometimes it's having someone's respect that changes his or her willingness to listen and get him or her to open up. Again, it's about finding your way to worth again.

The Corona virus came into our lives in 2020 and really either brought out the best in us or the worst in us. Hard times can do that. When faced with difficulty, ask yourself how you want to be remembered. My father had a funny line that had so much truth to it. He would say, "If you see only you, then get out of the mirror." This world is about helping each other, whether it be financially, spiritually, or maybe just in our daily growth. When you come to realize only life matters, you have learned one of life's greatest lessons. I always feel if you spend enough time with someone you keep a piece of them with you. I believe this has always helped me in my healing process. Don't underestimate what God has in store for you. He can deliver the light in the darkest clouds of doubt. They say you can learn more from a loss than you do through a victory. I have to say, I agree. Denis Waitley says, "Failure should be our teacher, not our undertaker. Failure is delay, not defeat. It is a temporary detour, not a dead end. Failure is something we can avoid only by saying nothing, doing nothing, and being nothing."

I would like to remind you to make sure you see your windows of opportunity. There are so many things that come our ways that can pull us out of the pit. Search for those things you can celebrate again or maybe look for something new. Maybe you buy a pet? Perhaps you go on vacation? Beginning a workout regime is always a great solution. There are so many ways you can put yourself on the right track. I wrote this book because I want everyone to get the most out of life. Again, leave the loss in the past, but keep the lessons you learned with you. Remember there is always something you can do about it. You need to flip the switch and make it happen. I think we take for granted who we select as a partner, who we select as friends. Things happen at times we don't choose them to happen. Sometimes we can't even anticipate them happening and we are left to deal with it. When we survive that initial blow, at that point we need to realize we are doing better than we were an hour ago. Don't stay in the bad mode. Get yourself in that better mode. There are times we walk around our problems, instead of walking right into them. We would rather allow pain to linger, because we refuse to change our pace. My faith pushes me forward and I know the lessons I will learn may not expose themselves right away. They say scars tell more stories, but that doesnt mean the book ends there. You are the author, so it's your job to write the next chapters or maybe even the next book. Distractions defeat us more than the obstacle itself.

I hope this book has helped you in some way. I try to get my story out there to help other people conquer their problems and show them that they can smile again. The people showcased in this chapter are just some of the people who made huge differences in not only my life, but in my healing as well.

All my best on a speedy recovery and a life surrounded with love, laughter and happiness!

Mike Terzi

On November 12, 2009, we lost my brother-in-law, Mike Terzi, at the age of forty. Mike was a huge sports fan. He loved the Yankees and Giants, and I'm glad he was able to see them win before he passed. I don't know if there was a happier man on Earth when the Giants beat the undefeated Patriots in 2007.

Mike's true passion, however, was coaching his kids, no matter what the sport was. Both Mike and I were asked to coach soccer because our children's coaches quit the night before the first game and we were the only ones who had coaching certifications. We both did it without really knowing the game. Mike studied the rules and came up with drills to make us a better team and give our players something on which to build. He always arrived at practice early and left late. He would always give credit where credit was due. That's the man he was. He was also the life of any holiday party or picnic because he was just a down-to-earth family man. Our sons were close in age, so Mike and I coached the boys together over the years. We enjoyed a lot of successful seasons and milestones. Mike was full of knowledge and passion, so he always came prepared to play. He would come to every game with a scouting report to put us all in a better place to win the game. He was just a happy guy who enjoyed life and knew what was most important in the world. It was a difficult call to take from my sister that morning of his passing. As I drove to the hospital, I thought about how he had prepared his sons for high school sports and now he would have to watch them from above. Time may have cheated him, but his huge heart was a great example for all of us.

Mike and I spent a lot of time together watching movies. He was a huge movie fan. We were even in an independent movie together. Words can't express how much that movie means to me now. He loved ball games and it didn't matter what sport. He always took an interest in your life and asked how everyone and everything was. He was always there for anyone in need, to listen or offer any type of comfort he could. He loved the holidays and would be one of the first to arrive and one of the last to leave celebrations. Mike knew what the important things were in life. He would work any job to provide for his family. There's so much he brought to my life that I don't know what I miss most about him. We talked every day and those conversations were mostly about how he could make his boys' lives better. Although he left us too soon, I hope he's looking down and seeing the huge impact he's had on all our lives. There isn't a holiday party that goes on without us mentioning a time when he made us smile and laugh. All I can say is that I miss you, Brother!!

Mike Terzi

Dennis Mannion

Dennis Mannion was my teacher and coach during my high school years. He is a hero of mine, and he is my friend. I believe God put us on the same path because of what we had in common and how we could help each other. I've learned so much about loss and overcoming not only from his stories as a Vietnam veteran, but also through the books he had us read in his English class. The main characters in those books always had something to overcome. We would always review the stories and compare them to real life stories. He gave you 100 percent and expected 100 percent from you. You always knew he had your back and your best interest in mind.

My junior year of football I broke my thumb. I was trying to find a way to get back on the field. Coach Mannion took my helmet and said, "Son, you have a lot of football in you, just not tonight." I went from wanting to get in the game to being fine with just cheering on my team that night. That's the level of trust I had for him. There was no doubt in my mind he was pointing me in the right direction.

He doesn't sugarcoat anything, he says it like it is. That is refreshing in this day and age. I learned from him as a player, as a student, and mostly as a person. He backed what he spoke and that, to this day, inspires me to always do my best. He never judges people on their mistakes, but on how they respond to those mistakes. I have been out of school for almost thirty years and I still keep in contact with coach Mannion. He continues to steer my life in a positive direction, by telling me what books to read or coming on my talk show and sharing his stories with my viewers.

One story that stands out in my memory is the time he stayed and read to his former student Jay Escoto. Jay had been ill since his childhood and had limited time with us and his one request was that Mr. Mannion read to him. He stayed the night with him so he could read at any moment Jay felt up to it. That story is embedded in my heart and something I will never forget. Mr. Mannion and I talk a few times a year on the phone and every once in a while we grab lunch together, but either way I always hear great stories from a great man. I learned so much from this man and I still use what I learned to this day.

Dennis Mannion

Coach Mannion wrote this about me my senior year and it still means a lot to me. Never underestimate what a page of meaningful words can do for someone.

February 25, 1990

To Whom It May Concern,

I have been asked to write on behalf of Bill Gannon, and I am pleased to be able to do so. I have known him since his sophomore year of high school, and I have coached him on the football field and taught him in the classroom. The focus of this letter, however, will be with football and Billy's ability in that area.

I coached Billy in the fall of 1988 when he was the starting quarterback on the varsity team. Even though I was not his "position-coach," it was clear to me that he had a love for the game that one does not see in a lot of players today. There were numerous times that fall (and since) that I felt that his genuine affection for the game rivaled mine when I was a high school player. Today's players operate in a society that is much different from the one that existed when I played (1960 to 1966), but when I look at Billy and his approach to the game, I see myself. I did not ever have the talents that he possessed, but like him, football was the world I lived in and not much else mattered. Whether it was the excitement of game day or tedious, numbing mid-week practice, Billy accepted and soared in all of it. He was always ready to work, always willing to jump in when an extra body was needed, and always the player you had to order off the field because it was time to stop throwing footballs and go home for dinner.

Billy certainly had a future as a college quarterback; his throwing ability alone was as good as I have seen in sixteen years of being an assistant coach on the high school level. I can't say how far his talents would have taken him, but with a year of prep school, his desire to exceed, and his obvious work habits, he might have played competitively on any college level. His skill was that good.

I was not a football coach in the fall of 1989, and as such, I am not qualified to write about his senior year football experience. I can say that his love for the sport was evident in many conversations we had prior to the start of English class. Billy remains competitive, industrious, and he certainly is an example of what sportsmanship is all about. I know that he misses football; football certainly misses him.

Sincerely,

Dennis M. Mannion
English Dept.
Mark T. Sheehan High School

Maryann Gannon

I never knew how strong my mother was until a year before her death when she told us she had dealt with a private, painful issue since she was a child. I marveled at how she was able to mask her own pain so we could grow up without judgment. That was a true sign of a mother's love.

My mother loved to cook and made holidays very special for anyone who came. I still hear people say how they enjoyed the things she cooked or baked. She didn't have much growing up, she had a very humble upbringing. Kindness stood out most with her character. She could calm a crying child in a heartbeat. My mother only asked one thing of me, to never give up my faith. I was blessed to have her remind me of that when I needed it most. She told me once how she prayed every day for all her children. I bet that saved me a time or two in my journey. She put others' needs in front of her own. She taught me the pay-it-forward way of life. She gave us all so much. She had a combination of caring and sharing that very few people possess today. She was the biggest fan of her children and grandchildren. She showed us how simple acts could mean so much. Whether it was the meals she made, the art she drew, or just a walk through the amazing flower garden she created for all of us to enjoy, she made a difference. She always told me to be involved in my grandparent's lives because we never knew when we would lose the people around us.

My mother's strength was never more apparent than at the end of her life, when she was more worried about the direction of our lives then hers. Words can't express the amount of love I received from my mother from the day I was born to the day she passed. How do you say thank you to someone who has given you so much? I remember her being so proud that Danielle's middle name was Mary, after her. I have this love for movies because of my mother; she would always rent me two movies when I was home sick. She was always there for all of us from the day we were born until the day she passed away. I can only think of how great my childhood was. I made my family face a lot of hard times, especially my parents, but they just kept showing me that love that is unbreakable.

My mother and daughter Casey. My mother had a way of always making her grandchildren happy.

William James Gannon

My father was a huge influence in my life. I learned most of my lessons from him first hand, that's just the way he was. It was more than just words with my father, he wouldn't just say it, he'd do it. Growing up as a child I couldn't believe how many people looked up to him because of what he could do on a ball field or basketball court. He wasn't loved just for his athletic abilities, though. As I grew, I saw that he was loved more because of his heart and the way he treated people. My father was a big believer in the underdog. He asked only for your best, no matter what that was.

My father never made excuses. Somehow, some way, he got it done, and he expected the same from those around him. . The impossible always seemed to become possible in all things he did. My father also had an amazing work ethic and never complained. He worked as a salesman during the day and owned a cleaning company at night. One of the most important things he taught me was how to be a gentleman. Every Valentine's Day my father would buy my mother and my four sisters boxes of chocolates. It was never about himself. I can now appreciate how much he gave to me though I really didn't see how meaningful it was until I became a father. His go-to saying was, "The older you get, the wiser I'll be." He was right.

My father relished the little things in life. He would take us out to family dinners on Saturday nights. He loved hosting holiday parties or just Sunday picnics to get us all in one place together. He would play Waylon Jennings and Willie Nelson records, and enjoy every minute of it. He always showed us how important that time together was.

Now that I'm older, I can see how much my mother and father sacrificed for my sisters and me. I just hope I can be half the parent that my parents were for me. This is a picture of them enjoying each other's company in Cape Cod, Massachusetts.

Joe Kurcaba

It wouldn't be possible to write this part of the book and not include my long-time friend, Joe Kurcaba. Joe has been my friend through so many of my difficult times. We met in fourth grade and was a staple in my life when we were growing up. I'll never forget the day I first met him. He was outside in his yard shooting a snake with a BB gun. That was the start of tree forts, riding cows, and driving his grandmother's car when she wasn't home. We never really had to look for trouble, most of the time it found us, but we'll keep those stories for another book. I'm just glad we were never hurt worse than we were, with all of our adventures.

Joe has a great heart and always puts others' needs in front of his own. I have learned a lot from him and his father. Even though we went to different high schools, Joe and I remained close. He was over my house almost every day after the car accident. We watched a lot of movies. Trust me when I tell you we could quote most movies, especially *Jaws, Star Wars*, or *Raiders of the Lost Ark.* There were many holidays, family gatherings, and Monday-night football games we were able to share. We still catch a movie or dinner together here and there to catch up and laugh about our past. I know if I called and needed him, he'd be at my door within the hour. I would do the same for him. I couldn't ask for a better friend, and I thank God for giving me such a great person to call friend. Joe is always looking to make this world a better place for everyone around him.

Joe Kurcaba

Leon Z Klopocki

Leon was my father-in-law and I was lucky to know him. I learned so much from this gentleman. He would always kiss a woman's hand and he was one of the best dancers I ever saw. He was a hard-working man who would leave before any of us were awake and come home long after we were already there. The biggest gift I received from Leon was the lesson of unconditional love.

My wife Agnes was his stepdaughter, but he loved her like his own blood. He opened my eyes to this way of living. He was just a jolly soul who opened his heart to whomever wanted to be his family or friend. He loved to play Lotto and played numbers that had meaning to him, such as birthdays and anniversaries.

Leon had a great will and work ethic. If he came home early from work saying he was feeling well, you knew he was really sick. He wouldn't miss a day of work for something minor. After undergoing a successful triple bypass surgery, he quit smoking, which had been a steady habit for him for years. He was never tempted by it again.

Leon showed me that a kind soul could exist in this world. Some people accomplish things with their head, but Leon's greatest accomplishments were done with his heart. He was one of those guys you could never thank enough. Although he never won the big prize in the lottery, he made the people around him feel as if they hit the jackpot. He showed me the right combination of love and laughter goes a long way.

Leon Klopocki enjoying life

Joe Kuczo

Throughout this book, I have mentioned my Uncle Joe numerous times. My uncle became a big factor in my life when I was in eighth grade and called him to tell him my dream of becoming a professional quarterback. From then on, he was with me every step of the way. He sent footballs, vitamins, videotapes, and all sorts of equipment to aid in my journey. Although my goal was not to be, our relationship continued. His life stories were very important for me both before and after my accident.

Uncle Joe had the ability to find the bright spot in any situation. He showed me he was more than just words when he suffered a stroke and tackled his injuries head on. I was most impressed when my aunt, his wife, fell sick and Joe's ailments took a backseat to hers. It was the true definition of a love story. Both were sick, so theirs wasn't your typical ending, but they fought together until they couldn't. That story alone taught me so much. Joe proved to not only myself but to everyone around him that true love conquers all.

I think of him often and I'm truly grateful for his love and guidance. When I was younger I thought he had given me all the tools to succeed in a profession, but I didn't quite realize that what he gave to me allowed me to succeed in life as well.

As a quarterback, you are the leader on the field. I remember like it was yesterday going into my freshman year of high school and my uncle saying to me, "Lead with your heart, head and humility, you'll find the players around you will be quick to follow. Then you will be able to lead with power and strength." He had a lifetime of wisdom to offer anyone willing to listen. I've heard from many of the Redskin players he coached about how conversations with my uncle were priceless and they were also happy to have him in his life. Uncle Joe could point out a weakness of yours, but always offered a unique way for you to conquer it. He was a master at getting you to see the progress and not the problem. His life was dedicated to serving and helping others no matter what life threw at them. Joe definitely gave more then he took. He was a great example and definitely someone who extended himself to his fellow humans.

Uncle Joe at Redskin Park with Vince Lombardi, probably offering words of wisdom.

Father Paul Hallovatch

I don't even know where to start when talking about Father Paul. I remember him inviting Matt Escoto and I to lunch a few weeks after we both got out of the hospital. I knew from that day on that he was a special priest with a gift to spread God's word and love. Whether offering a simple blessing or a celebrating Mass, Father Paul always seems to come up with the right words to comfort you and bring you closer to Jesus Christ. I have known him for more than thirty years and my life is better because of him.

Father Paul is a huge fan of UConn basketball, something he had in common with my dad. It was nice to have those conversations with Father Paul after I lost my dad. He also has one of the most impressive collections of crosses and other religious artifacts around, along with a prayer room that is second to none. He's given me oils and holy water that has not only helped me in my healing process, but others as well. It's a tough world to navigate through and I am truly blessed to have his guidance

Father Paul has a contagious laugh that can make anyone smile. I can say between Father Charles MacDonald and Father Paul they've both brought me so much closer to God. It was easy to follow them not only by their words or wisdom, but also mostly through their actions. We live in a world that's lost its moral compass and I've been more than blessed to have these two gentlemen helping me stay on the right track in life. Father Paul is now retired, but he still stays active in many ways to keep spreading the Word.

Father Paul has celebrated Christmas Mass at our house many times over the years. We are truly grateful for him.

Ron Garney

My friend Ron has been there for me for most of the tragic moments in my life, and I've been lucky to be able to bounce things off of him. Ron is very successful and his talent speaks for itself. Ron draws for Marvel Comics and for DC for a brief stint. Another artist told me he considers him the "Mickey Mantle" of comic book artists. He's also done storyboards for movies and has a show in development at the time. I had the pleasure of being part of a band, Ronin, which Ron created and for which he wrote songs and music. He was smart enough to keep me away from the microphone and instruments. He's a friend with whom you can have a deep conversation, but someone with whom laughter is always on deck. Ron is a martial arts master as well and a great husband and father, a job for which he doesn't get enough credit, at least from the people who didn't know him personally.

If you search Ron's name on the computer, it won't take long to see his talent. I can tell you many stories about Ron standing up for the underdog. He was someone I admired growing up as a teenager and having him in my life has been a blessing. He's definitely made me a better person and kept me on the right track. Ron is a friend who has always kept my best interests in mind and kept me away from those things that would or could alter my life in a negative way. His wisdom is worth the weight of gold.

Spending time with Ron is always fun and you never know what will happen or what topic will come up. I know he will say at some points that I would show up at times when he wanted to get his work done, but those were the times when important comic book issues came out and I was a big fan. I also know that if he could only spike his hair, he would.

Ron and I getting dinner together.

Jim Kelly

Another hero of mine was Hall-of-fame quarterback Jim Kelly. He was truly a role model for me and so many other players who dreamed of playing professional ball. . Jim Kelly had all the tools for success, but what was most impressive was his heart. He wouldn't give in no matter what the odds were. It was a pleasure to watch him play.

I attended his camp in the late eighties. He was at the top of his game, but very humble and willing to give back not only to the game he loved, but to his fans too. Jim took me under his wing at his camp that year and really stepped up my game in so many ways. He had me change my grip on the football, which allowed me to throw better spirals in the sun, rain, snow, or wind. After my car accident I received a handwritten letter from him. He wrote of an injury that almost sidelined him and almost kept him from playing football again. He told me to fight as hard as I could. A few years later we met up again at ESPN. He signed autographs and took pictures with my family. This meant a lot to us. Even though his playing career was now over by then, we saw how truly amazing his heart was.

Jim sadly lost his son, but started a foundation in his son's name to help others. He also was diagnosed with cancer in his upper jaw and his strength was sure front and center. One of the most heart-warming pictures I've seen was Jim's daughter lying on the hospital bed with him. It shows you what really matters in life.

Jim Kelly will always be linked to the Class of 1983, but most importantly he'll always be better known for being the class of the league. I've had the pleasure of seeing Jim on many different occasions and that smile comes right out. Jim's a hero who has lived up to his reputation, and in this day and age that's hard to come by. There are very few sports figures in today's game who can be considered role models for the younger generation, but Jim not only fits that bill, he well exceeds the expectations.

Hall of Fame Quarterback Jim Kelly and I

Dr. Francis X. Palermo

Dr. Palermo was my miracle maker from the moment he heard about me. After numerous doctors said I wouldn't walk for at least a year to possibly even two years, and one even wanted to amputate my leg that night of the accident, Dr. Palermo said he'd have me back on the football field by September. I bought into everything he said and he was right. At first he used the whole football return as motivation to at least get me moving in the right direction. As we got closer to the summer and things were moving toward a return, he never pulled back on any of the treatments. He was all in on completing this miracle. Even as he was being pressured by other doctors to keep me off the field, he stayed the course and was a man of his word. He was there for every game I was going to play. We pulled it off, with a lot of help from others. I wasn't the only one who needed this amazing doctor though. Dr. Palermo was eventually off to be a part of the Olympic team. I missed my doctor, but was blessed to have such a health provider.

Dr. Palermo not only healed, but offered hope as well. He came up with unusual treatments to aid with my return. I know he gave most of the credit for the return to me, but without his spark and knowledge it would have been just a dream. He's someone who can take a dream and make it reality. Dr. Palermo saw the person I was and not the problem I was facing. Doctors like this change people's lives. Even now at the age of seventy Dr. Palermo wants to keep providing patients with their best chance of healing. He never gives himself enough credit. To this day he tells me how amazing it was that I made it back to play football again. The truth is, I would have never come close to that dream without him and his unique way of treating me. He not only healed me physically, but maybe more so mentally.

Dr. Francis X. Palermo

Chris Selvaggi

There's a Gatorade commercial that talks about a rival who lifts your game. I never considered Chris Selvaggi a rival, I consider him a friend. Chris was built for overtime, there is no quit in him. He can change the atmosphere around him as he walks onto a field or into a gym or another establishment. I was lucky to call such a barrier breaker my friend. I truly believe he was put in my path of life to push me toward my goals. He always had my back on the field no matter what the situation was. He was that guy who always had another repetition or play in him. I remember summer training where we would push our bodies to the point of exhaustion, then you would look over toward him and he would say, "I have one more in me. Do you?" While Chris's goals were derailed by a back injury, he was a mountain of talent both on a baseball or football field. Chris now puts his focus and passion on the gym. Closing in on fifty years old, he keeps pushing the limits. He's pushing and pulling weights that most people can't do in their twenties. He showed me that you never give up on your goals. Even if one goal ends, you can make a new goal and put as much passion into that one.

Chris never recognized a plateau. If he hit one, he exploded right through it. At a point in my life when I was struggling to get myself back in shape, Chris called me a bunch of times with different routines that could assist with my recovery. It's been thirty years since I graduated and this guy hasn't given up on me yet. It's not crazy that we are still friends, but crazy we are still competitive with each other. He keeps my mind young by putting me in that frame of mind. We might be on the back nine when it comes to our lives, but we are far from backing down! You see when Chris pushes and pulls all these weights, he's pushing back at life and the odds. It's important the lessons others show us everyday. Chris posted a quote on social media the other day that said, "If my heart was for sale, you couldn't afford it." I can only hope everyone can have a friend like Chris in their life.

Chris Selvaggi and I, October 2019

Denise Cannata

When I think back to my freshman year of high school, I can't believe I passed Freshman English. All I heard going into this class was how hard it was. After my first day, however, I knew I would be okay. Mrs Cannata was a firm but fair teacher. She wasn't what I wanted (because I was lazy), but she was what I needed. She taught with a smile and passion second to none. Mrs Cannata saw my passion was football and she used that to push me in my academics. She taught her students how to improve themselves through education, which was a tough sell in my case.

Mrs. Cannata shoes can never be filled, because she was tailor-made for this job. The world today wouldn't allow a teacher of these standards , some who wanted the most out of you, no more, no less. She stayed on me until the day I graduated. My junior year, after the accident, I started my comeback to football and when I walked down her hallway and saw her, tears came down her eyes as she hugged me, I knew why she was so special. She had a son of her own, and the last thing she wanted was to see me go through pain again. When I think about her, I think of what an example she was for the girls in my class and all the others who were fortunate to have her in the classroom. It meant a lot to me that she was in attendance at my wedding, and I was so excited when I found out she would be teaching both Billy Jr. and Jeremy for their freshman years. She taught each student as if they were her only and as a parent you're so happy when your children get such a great foundation.

Jeremy witnessed her compassionate motherly side when he had a report due. It was during the time his grandmother was dying and her time was limited. We called Mrs. Cannata and explained the situation. Without hesitation she gave him more time and the support he needed at such a painful time. It's moments like those that forge a bond. That was the type of teacher she was. She gave her students a road map to navigate life and we are forever grateful.

Fern Pucciarello

Mrs. Pucciarello had a special way of getting the lesson through to her students. I met her during eighth grade. One day, my pencil kept breaking and I had to keep getting up to sharpen it. After the fifth time of sharpening it she sent me to the office. When I was at the office, I gave the principal the pencil to sharpen and I told him that if he could sharpen it then he could suspend me. The principal attempted to sharpen the pencil but wasn't successful. He sent me back to class with a note that vindicated me. After class she approached me concerning the incident and then things returned to normal. After that day she won my trust. I had two classes with her, and at this point we understood where we stood with each other. She had a gift of enabling her students to understand the true nature of intrinsic motivation. She motivated me by utilizing my love for football, by hanging the newspaper articles pertaining to my games on the wall. She made her students feel as if they all had a place in her heart and not just in the classroom.

It was her exam I took in the afternoon before my accident. We wished each other a nice weekend and I left, not knowing how my life would change. She didn't give up on me, though. She not only came to visit me in the hospital, but structured my studies to accommodate my situation. When I started my push to play football again, she remained positive. I was 126 pounds when I left the hospital and she used to bring strawberry milkshakes to me during our tutoring sessions. She always supported me and filled me in as to what was happening at school so I never felt left out. She made me a better student. She not only taught me about the subject, she also taught me something about myself. She had the ability to convince you of what you were capable of doing, even if you couldn't see it in yourself.

Epilogue

Life is too short! I bet you heard that somewhere before. We are all born with gifts. We all have a purpose for why we are here. Find your gifts and develop them and use them to the best of your abilities. Make your impact on this world regardless of what others think of you. Start moving people around you. Show off your gifts and teach those who respect their talent. Giving back will always make you better as well as helping others. There are dreams in all of us, it's up to us to see them become a reality. Everyday someone's dreams are coming true. Why can't it be yours? Make today that day that you stop sulking in your sorrows and start reaching for the stars. That does mean you're looking for fame, but that people just remember your name. Find that pivotal moment and push forward. I wish you all my best on your journey through this life.

Special Thanks to

MARING VISUALS

Charlie and Jennifer Maring always make me look good!
Maringvisuals.com

To my children, Casey, Billy and Jeremy. You are my blessings who keep me going!

I will never forget my friends, Marc Izzo and Matt Escoto, and the lessons they gave me. Rest in peace, my friends.

www.ingramcontent.com/pod-product-compliance
Lightning Source LLC
LaVergne TN
LVHW081317060426
835509LV00015B/1566

9780578687506